D0565757

Sock YARN STUDIO

Sock YARN STUDIO

HATS, GARMENTS, AND OTHER PROJECTS
DESIGNED FOR SOCK YARN

Featuring patterns from
Wendy D. Johnson,
Véronik Avery,
Franklin Habit,
and more

Carol J. Sulcoski

LARK CRAFTS
Asheville

EDITOR
Thom O'Hearn

DESIGNER
Kara Plikaitis

ART DIRECTOR
Megan Kirby

PHOTOGRAPHER
Carrie Hoge

TECHNICAL
ILLUSTRATIONS
Northfound, LLC

COVER DESIGNER
Kara Plikaitis

LARK CRAFTS

An Imprint of Sterling Publishing
387 Park Avenue South
New York, NY 10016

If you have questions or comments about
this book, please visit: larkcrafts.com

Library of Congress Cataloging-in-Publication Data

Sulcoski, Carol, 1965-
  Sock yarn studio : hats, garments, and other projects designed for sock yarn / Carol J. Sulcoski.
     p. cm.
  Includes bibliographical references and index.
  ISBN 978-1-4547-0285-6 (alk. paper)
  1. Knitting--Patterns. 2. Knitwear. 3. Socks. 4. Yarn. I. Title.
  TT825.S82 2012
  746.43'2--dc23

                                 2011047744

10 9 8 7 6 5 4 3 2

Published by Lark Crafts
An Imprint of Sterling Publishing Co., Inc.
387 Park Avenue South, New York, NY 10016

Text © 2012, Carol Sulcoski
Photography © 2012, Lark Crafts, an Imprint of Sterling Publishing Co., Inc.,
unless otherwise specified
Illustrations © 2012, Lark Crafts, an Imprint of Sterling Publishing Co., Inc.,
unless otherwise specified

Distributed in Canada by Sterling Publishing,
c/o Canadian Manda Group, 165 Dufferin Street
Toronto, Ontario, Canada M6K 3H6

Distributed in the United Kingdom by GMC Distribution Services,
Castle Place, 166 High Street, Lewes, East Sussex, England BN7 1XU

Distributed in Australia by Capricorn Link (Australia) Pty Ltd.,
P.O. Box 704, Windsor, NSW 2756 Australia

The written instructions, photographs, designs, patterns, and projects in this volume are intended
for the personal use of the reader and may be reproduced for that purpose only. Any other
use, especially commercial use, is forbidden under law without written permission of the
copyright holder.

Every effort has been made to ensure that all the information in this book is accurate. However,
due to differing conditions, tools, and individual skills, the publisher cannot be responsible for any
injuries, losses, and other damages that may result from the use of the information in this book.

Printed in Canada

All rights reserved

ISBN 13: 978-1-4547-0285-6

For information about custom editions, special sales, and premium and corporate purchases, please
contact Sterling Special Sales Department at 800-805-5489 or specialsales@sterlingpub.com.

For information about desk and examination copies available to college and university professors,
requests must be submitted to academic@larkbooks.com. Our complete policy can be found at
www.larkcrafts.com.

Contents

preface

WHEN I FIRST RETURNED to knitting as an adult, I had no idea that I would end up fascinated with—some might say obsessed by—sock yarn. To my inexperienced knitting eyes, sock yarns seemed so skinny and slow to knit compared with heavier yarns, and the small needles used to knit with them felt like toothpicks.

At some point I gave in, intrigued by the enthusiasm of the many sock knitters I met. To my surprise, I found the process of sock knitting to be addicting: There's something ingenious about the process of crafting a garment that so perfectly fits the oddly-shaped human foot. As I joined sock knitters' message boards and bought books of sock patterns, I learned about a category of yarn that I'd previously ignored.

I discovered beautiful hand-painted yarns, crafted by artisans who sampled every color of the rainbow in a single skein. I found self-patterning yarns that made stripes, checks, and other patterns like magic, without the knitter ever needing to change a ball of yarn. I encountered yarns made with silk, bamboo, tencel, sea cell, cotton, even Australian possum fur. Heathers and tweeds; subtly-dyed, nearly-solid colors; barber pole striped—there seemed to be no end to the variety of sock yarns out there.

As my infatuation with sock yarn reached its peak, I found I had amassed a rather large stash of sock yarns

in a relatively short period of time. Although I still enjoyed knitting socks, it seemed natural to wonder what else I might be able to do with all the sock yarn I had lovingly collected.

I thought about all the advantages that sock yarn had when it came to knitting socks—the lightweight fabric it created, the machine-washability, the nearly infinite variety and gorgeous colors. Why not see how those qualities applied to knitting other items as well? It turned out that a ball or two of sock yarn was the perfect amount for a hat or scarf. The relatively fine gauge of sock yarn created airy lace and garments that could be worn three seasons of the year (I'm still trying to figure out summer). The machine-washability and durability of many sock yarns made them ideal for knitting baby items.

Naturally this only increased my desire for more sock yarn! As time went by, I kept adding sock yarns to my stash, and then I began dyeing and selling sock yarns. Even today, when I go to a fiber show or a new knitting shop, I'm almost irresistibly drawn to the sock yarn section, ever on the lookout for a new brand, a funky fiber blend, or an enticing colorway to add to my stash.

All of this is a long way of explaining why I decided to write this book. In short, I wanted to create something that celebrates the joys of sock yarn—and emphasizes how ideal it is for knitting things *other than* socks!

This book is intended first and foremost for my fellow knitters equally obsessed with sock yarn, with a selection of fun and good-looking patterns designed especially for the sock yarn they love and collect. But I also hope this book will win some new converts. Maybe you're a seasoned sock knitter who has knit bunches of socks and is ready to try something new (without buying a whole new stash). Maybe you don't have any desire to knit socks—or you live in a climate where sandals are more practical than socks—but you find yourself tempted by the beautifully-colored skeins and wild patterns of today's sock yarns. Maybe you're an accessories knitter, preferring to work on projects that are smaller than full-size sweaters. Maybe you're relatively new to knitting and need a gentle nudge in the sock yarn direction.

Whatever kind of knitter you are, I invite you to pull up a comfy chair, surround yourself with your stash, and dive into this book. You'll never look at sock yarn in the same way again.

Disclaimers

Before we get into the real knitting stuff, let's talk about what is and isn't in this book.

This book is devoted to the joys of sock yarn—but for knitting items *other than* socks. That means you won't find any sock patterns in this book. Not a single one. If you are looking for sock patterns, there are many beautiful sock knitting books out there—but don't expect to see any sock patterns here. (Do you hear me? Absolutely none!)

This book is designed for someone who already knows the basics of knitting. If you don't yet know how to knit, this book isn't going to teach you. There are many wonderful "learn how to knit" books out there. If you are a new knitter, though, don't worry; the patterns in this book cover a range of skill levels.

This book focuses on fingering-weight sock yarns. We'll talk about this in more detail later, but suffice it to say that the vast majority of patterns in this book were designed to work with the classic, fingering-weight sock yarn, rather than heavier weights of yarn.

In picking the yarns used for this book, the other designers and I have attempted to sample all of the delights of the sock yarn world. You'll find projects that use commercially-dyed sock yarns, like Westminster Fiber's Regia, and projects knit in hand-dyed yarns, like Koigu and Madelinetosh. You'll find projects in solid yarns, nearly-solid hand dyes, machine-dyed variegated yarns, kettle-dyed yarns, hand-painted and self-patterning yarns. You'll find sock yarns made by big companies like Skacel as well as teeny tiny companies, like my own Black Bunny Fibers. You'll find all-wool choices; wool-nylon blends; and other fiber combinations incorporating silk, bamboo, or cashmere. More importantly, I hope seeing different kinds of yarns used (and in some cases, combined) will give you the confidence to select the yarns and colors that you love.

UNDERSTANDING
Sock
YARN

Whether you're new to knitting with sock yarns or already know and love them, this chapter will help you avoid some common mistakes, give you tips for selecting the kind of sock yarn that will produce the results you want, and increase your pleasure in knitting with the sock yarn you already have.

what is "sock yarn"?

IN THE BROADEST SENSE, any yarn that is used to knit socks is a kind of "sock yarn." Many years ago, in a world where the only yarns you had were the ones you spun yourself, knitters didn't have much choice when it came to knitting socks. They took the wool from their own sheep, spun it on a wheel or spindle, and used it to knit socks. Maybe those socks were bulky or itchy, and they certainly weren't machine washable (washing machines having not yet been invented), but they did the essential job of keeping feet warm.

Over time, more yarns were manufactured by machines. As mill-made yarns became available and affordable, knitters began to develop opinions about the best types of yarn to use for knitting socks. Warmth was still essential, but durability was important, too, since socks are subjected to so much friction from the odd angles of a foot and the insides of a shoe. As washing machines became popular, sock yarns that could be washed by machine, rather than by hand, became desirable. Eventually, technological advances made machine-knit socks more affordable than handknit ones. As sock knitting became a hobby rather than a necessary part of housekeeping, appealing to a knitter's whimsy and color sense began to take precedence over more practical concerns. Thus, in recent years, we've seen the introduction of luxury fibers and artisanal yarns to further tempt knitters into wanting to knit socks rather than buying mass-made ones at the store.

Today, most knitters and yarn companies use the phrase "sock yarn" loosely to refer to all sorts of yarn that is marketed for the primary purpose of knitting socks. That means that a wide variety of yarns may say "sock yarn" on the label, simply because the manufacturer intends for the yarn to be used for socks. Most of these yarns have certain things in common—qualities that make them particularly appropriate for knitting socks:

- Most are designed to be machine-washable and resist felting

- Most use wool breeds, fiber blends, and plied construction to make them durable, resist pilling, and reduce damage from friction

- Most are fingering-weight so that they will fit inside a shoe without excess bulk

- Most are soft and feel good against your skin

TOP: This sock yarn is a favorite of mine for its soft hand, vivid colors, unusual color combinations, and color transitioning. But from a strict yarn construction standpoint, yarns made like this one aren't ideal for socks. The yarn is single-ply and rather softly twisted, making it less durable than multi-ply and tightly twisted yarns. The trade-off? Buttery softness and super-pleasant knitting.

BOTTOM: Here are some gorgeous hand-painted sock yarns that are not machine washable. I'm happy to wash them by hand, in cold water, with minimum agitation, to make sure they won't shrink or felt.

Indeed, when many knitters think of sock yarn, they think of the classic sock yarns—workhorse yarns like Regia, Trekking, Opal, Fortissima and others. These yarns are fingering weight; consist of multiple strands that are tightly twisted together; usually incorporate nylon, polyamide, or other manmade fibers for durability; resist felting; are machine washable; and are made mainly of wool. If you go to a yarn shop and ask for sock yarn, you are likely to be shown an enticing display of these classics.

You may have noticed that in the list above, I qualified my answers by saying, "most." Most sock yarns are fingering weight, machine-washable, tightly spun and plied, and so on. But not *all* yarns that are called "sock yarns" or are marketed to sock knitters have all of these qualities. Indeed, some of my favorite sock yarns don't meet all of these criteria.

Like just about everything else in life, with yarn there are sometimes trade-offs. That doesn't make any of these yarns bad or inferior; it just means you have to consider their advantages and disadvantages when deciding when to use them. (I'll give you some tips on doing that later in this section.) For now, trust me when I say that just as Barbara Woodhouse has never met a bad dog, I have never met a bad sock yarn. It's all in the handling.

categorizing sock yarn

FOR THE PURPOSES OF this book, I've chosen to divide the universe of sock yarns into categories based on how they're made and how they behave when you're knitting with them. All sock yarns can be sorted into the following general categories:

1. Solid sock yarns

2. Self-patterning sock yarns

3. Multicolored sock yarns

Let's consider them one by one.

SOLID SOCK YARNS

Solid yarns are, as you've no doubt guessed, yarns that are dyed in one color that is uniform throughout the skein.

The majority of solid sock yarns are dyed by machine at a mill or a dye-house. By dyeing yarn in large quantities, rather than in individual skeins by hand, yarn manufacturers produce yarns that are very consistent in color. As you can see in the photo on page 13, all of the yarn in the skein is the same color, and overall, the shade remains pretty consistent from one batch or dye lot to the next.

Every once in a while, particularly at a sheep show or fiber fair, you might encounter a solid-colored yarn that isn't dyed. Sheep's wool comes in different colors—white, cream, brown, beige, gray, black—and if a farm or mill processes that wool without bleaching or dyeing it, the end product will be yarn in those natural colors. Often these yarns will be marketed as "natural" or "undyed." They may also be labeled with the particular breed of sheep that produced the wool, like "Jacob," "Cormo," or "Shetland."

I'm also including yarns that might more accurately be called "nearly solid" in the solid category. Consider the gorgeous yarns used for the Autumn Walking Scarf. These yarn aren't 100 percent uniform in color—the lightness and darkness of the shades vary somewhat throughout the skein. Yarns like these might, if we were being nitpicky, more accurately be called "nearly solid" or even "semi-solid." If you squint your eyes or step back and look at them, they read as solids, but take a closer look and you can see some minor changes in color.

LEFT: Shown here are several different types of solid-colored sock yarn.

CENTER: Even though the yarns used in the Autumn Walking Scarf are nearly solid rather than completely uniform in color, they work beautifully in stranded colorwork. Indeed, the minor variations in color add depth and interest to the pattern.

RIGHT: See how the solid yarn used in the Vert Cap shows off the intricate lace pattern to perfection.

Why might a yarn be a semi-solid or nearly solid?

- It might be a tweed, in which flecks of other-colored yarns are spun into the surface of the base yarn.

- It might be hand-dyed, where subtle differences within one color are deliberately created by the artisan by changing the saturation or precise shade of the dye.

- It might be kettle-dyed, where dye in the kettle or vat adheres more to some sections of the yarn than to others, making sections of the yarn darker or lighter.

- It might be made from fibers that started out as different colors rather than uniform white (for example, wool taken from sheep that are white, light gray, and beige in color).

- It might be made of a blend of different fibers that take dye or reflect light differently.

Generally I've found that nearly-solids and semi-solids will behave enough like true solid yarns to be treated the same. The subtle differences in color or shade will not affect the way these yarns are used in the patterns, and so I've put them together in the same category.

Solid (and semisolid and nearly solid) yarns are the workhorses of the sock yarn world. Fancy stitchwork—lace, cables, texture—is shown off beautifully, without any clashes of color to interfere with your eye's appreciation of it. Solids play well with others, whether used with other solids or to tone down a multicolored yarn. If you aren't sure what kind of yarn to use, selecting a solid is your safest bet. While these yarns may not have the zing of some of the more vivid or multihued sock yarns, they will handle all sorts of patterns beautifully. They are classics that will stand the test of time.

SELF-PATTERNING (INCLUDING SELF-STRIPING) SOCK YARNS

One of the most fascinating developments for sock yarn is the invention of yarns that—seemingly by magic, with only a single ball of yarn and minimal effort by the knitter—create stripes, jacquards, and fair isle patterns. It's hard to tell when looking at the skein, but when knit up, these yarns create intricate patterns.

Self-patterning yarns can be made using a variety of processes, but all have one thing in common: The knitter just keeps knitting, while the yarn does all the work. It's hard to come up with a word besides "magical" to describe the process. The yarn changes from one color to the next by itself, without the knitter joining a different ball. There are no charts to follow or extra ends to weave in. You just knit away, and when you're done, you've got stripes, jacquards, or other fascinating patterns.

Different types of self-stripers produce very different effects. Some stripers make very wide but distinct bands of color (such as the Poems Sock yarn used in the Compostela Scarf). Some make very narrow stripes (such as the Lorna's Laces colorway used for the sleeves of the child's Gumdrop Raglan). Some create a mix of stripes, some thin, some wide, some medium-width (you can see these in several of the blocks of the Lizalu Blanket). Some mix little checks or other box-like patterns in with stripes (like the Opal colorway used in the Calico Scarf). Some seem to morph almost imperceptibly from one color to the next, changing one ply at a time.

BELOW: The Peacock Cap mixes a self-striper dyed in different shades of red with a solid black yarn, creating a multihued effect with only two balls of yarn.

ABOVE: While the patterning of the Calico Scarf looks complex, it was created entirely with one ball of yarn, in plain stockinette stitch. The specially-dyed yarn did all the work.

Self-patterning yarns are terrific for knitting spectacular looking socks with a minimum of fuss. But they can be great fun to use for other, non-sock garments, too—where they provide lots of color changes without the extra expense of buying multiple skeins of yarns in different colors. They are also wonderful for stranded knitting. By using one skein of a self-striper and one of a solid yarn, you get ever-changing rows of color almost effortlessly.

MULTICOLORED SOCK YARNS

If you take out the solids and the self-patterning sock yarns, what's left? The multicolors, of course! For the purposes of this book, I've defined "multicolor" to include all yarns with more than one color in them *except* for those deliberately designed to create stripes or patterns. That's a big category, and includes multicolored hand-dyed (also called "hand-painted" yarns), marled yarns, and space-dyed yarns. Space-dyed yarns (what my mother calls "variegated" yarns) are one type of multicolored yarn created by machine, rather than dyed by hand. Marled yarns are the ones that have a barber pole effect: They are made by combining two or more strands or plies of yarn that are different colors. When the different-colored plies are twisted together, they spiral around each other, creating that distinctive candy-striped look.

Multicolored yarns, especially hand-dyed ones, have increased in popularity in the past few years. Why are knitters so fascinated by multicolored yarns? Well, the appeal of capturing multiple colors in one skein of yarn is one reason—in just a minute or so, the knitter can work her way from one end of the rainbow to the other, all within a single skein of yarn. Space-dyed yarns, dyed by machine rather than by hand, are a particularly cost-effective way to achieve multihued effects. The growth of artisanal yarns is another factor; certain dyers have rabid followings because they so masterfully combine hues, with each skein or colorway an individual work of art.

While using multicolored yarns is certainly fun, these yarns also present certain challenges. Chief among them is pooling—the tendency of colors to creates stripey, splotchy, or other undesired effects (see pages 19-20). Sometimes multicolored yarns which look one way in the skein look different when knit up, and knitters with a more restrained style can find them overwhelming to wear.

Because multicolored yarns already combine colors (often in striking ways), the general rule for them is to stick with simpler patterns, letting the yarn's colors shine through. Many knitters find that complex stitch patterns, like intricate lace or cables, can be overwhelmed by the multiple hues, with the eye being drawn to the colors of the yarn, rather than the beauty of the stitchwork. If you're unsure about a particular multicolored yarn, or you've played around with it and aren't crazy about how it knits up, combining a multicolored yarn with a solid yarn can help tone it down.

The Chambourcin Halter features a very subtle hand-painted yarn knit on its own, while the women's version of the Alexander Street Cap tones down the color changes of a multicolored hand-paint by alternating it with a solid.

ᕙ repeats ᕣ

YOU MAY HAVE HEARD other knitters refer to a yarn's "repeat" and wondered exactly what they meant. Understanding the concept of a yarn's repeat is critically important when you're working with multicolored sock yarns. So let's take a closer look at what a yarn's repeat is, and why it matters.

The word "repeat" is defined as something that recurs or happens again. And a yarn's repeat is a sequence of colors that you'll encounter over and over again in a ball of multicolored yarn. To understand exactly where a yarn's repeat comes from and how it works, it helps to think about the way in which yarns are dyed. Let's start by looking at how most hand-painted yarns are made.

Before a hand-dyer can apply dye to a yarn, she first has to wind off the yarn into a hank. (A hank is a quantity of yarn wound into an oval shape, usually tied at several places to avoid tangling.) If you look at the hank in the photo on page 18, or spread out one of your own hanks of yarn on a table in front of you, you can see how the hank consists of many oval loops of yarn. All the loops run in the same direction, and the individual strands in each loop run parallel to one another. All the individual loops are about the same size, too, since they were created by being wound around a stationary object, like a niddynoddy or the arms of a wooden winder. Usually a hank is about two yards in circumference, meaning that each individual loop of yarn in the hank measures two yards around. (Different dyers may work with slightly different sized hanks ranging from 48 to 72 inches/122 to 183cm in circumference, but the most common size is about 72 inches/183cm.)

As the dyer applies dye to the hank, she creates segments of color. She may apply segments of, say, red, then switch colors and apply segments of orange, then switch colors again and create segments of gold. She may leave segments undyed, so that they stay white, or she may overlap colors, creating new colors where the two dyes mix together. She may make all the individual color segments the same length, or she may vary the length of individual color segments, making some longer, others shorter. Regardless of the precise method or style, however, she applies color in a series of segments that circle around the oval hank. Because the individual yarn strands are parallel to each other, each individual strand contains the same color segments in the same order. And that pattern of color segments is the yarn's repeat.

Multicolored yarns that are dyed by machine rather than by hand may also contain a repeat. Methods of commercial yarn dyeing vary (for example, dyes may be sprayed onto yarn strands or applied to machine-knit fabric that is later unwound), but no matter what method is used, if a recurring pattern of colors is applied to the yarn over and over again, the yarn will have a repeat. Self-striping yarns have a repeat; when you look at the yarn knit up into a garment, you can see how the color and often width of the stripes form a regular, repeating pattern. Likewise, self-patterning yarns like Regia and Opal also have a recurring sequence of colors and patterns forming their repeats.

One last note about repeats: A yarn's repeat can vary greatly in length. Most hand-painted yarns have repeats that are the same size as the hank in which the yarn was wound when it was dyed (most often around two yards), with individual color segments ranging from one to six inches. But some yarns, particularly self-striping yarns that include many colors or are designed to make wide stripes, have individual color segments that stretch on for yards, making the length of the skein's repeat very long.

In the example shown below, the hank of yarn has been dyed with the following color segments, in this order: brown, brick red, purple, pink, brown, brick red, brown, pink, purple, brick red. That pattern is the repeat for this hank of yarn.

REPEATS AND POOLING

When I teach knitting classes, no matter what the topic, the one question I get asked time and time again is, "Why do hand-painted yarns pool?" Pooling—the way multicolored yarns knit up to create masses of color in odd or unattractive ways—is one of the perils of multicolored yarns, particularly hand-dyed yarns.

The hand-dyed yarn used for the sleeves of the Gumdrop Raglan pools somewhat, but the effect is charming for the sleeves of a child's sweater.

Whether a yarn pools and to what extent it does is a direct result of the yarn's repeat. We saw in the previous section how some yarns, particularly hand-painted ones, have a recurring pattern of color segments. This concept sounds a bit abstract when you are merely looking at a sample hank of yarn. But think about what would happen if you began knitting with that hank of yarn. As you knit, the working yarn is continually used to make the stitches you create. The color of the stitches will follow the exact pattern of the yarn's repeat. If you began to knit with a strand of the sample skein shown on page 18, your first stitches would be brown as you knit the yarn from the first brown segment. The next group of stitches would be brick red (the second segment), then purple (the third segment), then a few stitches in pink, a few in brown, a few in brick red, a few in brown, then pink, then purple. At that point, you'd have knit your way through one full repeat of the colors in that skein. If you continued knitting, you would begin the pattern all over again, knitting with each color segment, in order, working you way through the repeat over and over again.

After you work your way through a number of repeats, you may find that your stitches begin to stack up in patterns. If you are knitting in the round, as for a sock or hat, your stitches will be laid out in a series of circles that sit on top of each other, going around and around as you knit round after round. If you are knitting flat, your stitches will lay on top of each other in rows as you knit back and forth. Either way, the individual color segments, now knit into stitches, may begin to stack up in patterns. Depending on a myriad of factors, segments of the same color may end up sitting next to each other. This creates unusual, to many people unattractive, splotches of color—what knitters refer to as pooling. In other cases, different color segments end up sitting next to other colors in a regular or semi-regular pattern. This can also create odd-shaped patterns that are visible when you step back and look at the knitting. (Sometimes your knitting will create uncannily consistent patterns as different color segments lie next to each other in repeating patterns, making stripes, zigzags, or other shapes that are remarkably regular.) The pooling and other patterning are simply the result of the basic geometry of the repeat interacting with the rate at which the yarn is being knitted.

how you can avoid pooling

ONCE A KNITTER UNDERSTANDS why pooling happens, her next question is usually, "Is there any way to avoid pooling?" Yes and no. Some yarns will pool no matter what you do. It's just the way they were made. Others may pool in some projects but not others. If you've got a stubborn pooler, and you don't like the way it's knitting up, you can try any of the following strategies:

* Change your needle size. By changing the size of your stitches, you will use up each repeat at a different rate, which may be enough to change the way that individual color segments present in the finished object.

* Change your stitch pattern. Just as changing needle size can change the rate at which you use up your yarn, so can changing your stitch pattern. Slipped stitches can be especially effective in minimizing pooling, since the slipped stitches are not knit with the working yarn and remain their original color, further jumbling up the color pattern.

* Change the number of stitches you cast on. Again, changing the size of the finished knitting will shuffle the color segments in a different way, often reducing or eliminating pooling.

* Start knitting at a different place in the repeat. You might be surprised by how effective this can be at changing the way the color segments line up, thereby minimizing pooling and splotching.

* Try alternating two skeins (or mini-skeins) of the yarn. Knit one or two rows/ rounds in one skein, then the next one or two in a different skein (starting at a different place in the repeat).

* Consider alternating your hand-paint skein with another skein to create stripes. Alternating a hand-paint with a solid yarn can help tone down the wild color patterns of the hand-paint. Alternating two hand-paints in different colorways is riskier, since it's harder to predict whether the colors will clash or accentuate each other, but if you pick the colorways carefully and are lucky, you can create some striking effects that minimize the pooling of the individual skeins.

* If these tips don't work, you may want to put the yarn away, and use it for a different project. Sometimes a particular yarn interacts with a particular project in such a way that there is no getting around pooling, while using the yarn in a different pattern—particularly one especially designed with hand-paints in mind—yields lovely results.

REPEATS AND SELF-PATTERNING YARNS

While the subject of repeats most often arises in the context of hand-painted yarns and pooling, repeats are also critically important when it comes to knitting with self-patterning yarns. Let's consider self-striping yarns first.

In the previous section, we saw how a yarn's repeat can vary in length, and that hand-painted yarns tended to have relatively small repeats, of about two yards or so in length (or whatever the circumference of the hank in which they were wound). We also saw that self-striping yarns tend to have longer repeats made up of very long segments of a single, unbroken color, followed by another relatively long repeat of one color, followed by another long repeat, and so on.

As you begin knitting, you work all your new stitches using the first color segment. Because the color segment is long, you can complete at least one full row or round, often more, before the color changes. When the color changes, the stripe changes, and you continue knitting at least one full row/round in the second color. Because you are knitting full rows or rounds, the unbroken colors line up to create stripes.

As a general rule of thumb, the longer an individual segment of color is in a skein, the wider the stripe will be. (If you think about the way yarn makes stripes, this makes sense: The longer the color segments, the more rows or rounds you can knit in that color before it changes. The more rows or rounds you knit, the wider the stripe.) Conversely, the shorter the segment is, the thinner the stripe. (You'll knit fewer rows or rounds before the color changes, creating thinner stripes.) For a yarn to truly stripe, however, the color segment has to be long enough for the knitter to work at least one complete row or round before the color changes. If the segments are shorter than that, you'll get "near stripes," what look like a tiger's markings.

Yarns that create fair isle, jacquard, or more complex patterns do so based on the same principles. Very clever fiber engineers figure out the approximate

circumference of the average sock, and about how much yarn is required to work through one round of an average sock. Using computers, they apply dye in specific segments that have been calculated to create the desired pattern. If you were to stretch out a self-patterning yarn, you might see smaller segments of color that will create checked or vee patterns, then a couple of long segments of color that create stripes, then more short segments for checks, and so on. Because it takes a lot of work and experimentation to calculate exactly the size and order of segments to create the desired pattern, self-patterning yarns tend to be more expensive than other sock yarns.

When you're working with self-patterning yarns, keep a couple of things in mind. Because the stripes or other effects are created by the yarn's repeat, if you aren't pleased with the way the yarn is knitting up you can use the first four tips from the previous section to shuffle the color segments in a slightly different way. Just a small change in the number of stitches or needle size can make the pattern in one of these yarns go from messy to precise. Likewise, changing the rate at which you use up the yarn can alter the size of the stripes, or change the striping pattern from tiger near-stripes to perfect stripes. You'll have to play around a bit to achieve the best results for your project and yarn.

Here's where your knowledge about yarn repeats will stand you in good stead. Since self-patterning yarns tend to have a regular repeat, you can figure out the order of the stripe colors or patterned sections. In the photo shown above, you can readily see the repeat of this particular self-striping yarn: light orange stripe, deep orange stripe, yellowy orange stripe, gold stripe, chartreuse stripe, green stripe, aqua stripe, and so on, eventually starting at the beginning with yellow again. You can also see the repeat of a self-patterning yarn, like the one used in the Calico Scarf, tracing how the repeat begins with pink, then switches to a thinner band of orange, then a thin band of gray, thin band of pink, wide band of orange, wide band

You can see from this photograph how this particular ball of sock yarn has been dyed using fairly regular—but relatively long—segments of color. We've stretched out each individual color segment to show you how. If you knit with this yarn, you would begin knitting at the left, where the yarn is dyed light orange. You'd knit several rows or rounds with light orange, and then the yarn would change to darker orange. You'd knit several rows or rounds with darker orange, and then the yarn would change to gold, then chartreuse, then green, then blue-green, aqua, and so on. Every time the color changes, you'd have enough yarn to knit several rows or rounds, and then it would change. Voilá! Stripes.

of gray, speckled band, and so on, until you get back to the beginning and start with the first pink stripe again.

You can use your knowledge of the yarn's repeat to manipulate the pattern that results in the finished project. Many sock knitters do this in order to create two identical socks in self-striping yarn. When a knitter casts on for the first sock, she makes a note of the place in the repeat where she started. When she is finished with the first sock and ready to cast on the second, she looks for the same approximate point in the repeat to begin. (Often this requires that the knitter wind off a section of yarn in order to get to the desired point in the repeat.) This technique will work for any type of project in which consistency in the colors is important to the knitter. For example, when knitting the Thornapple Wrist Warmers, designer Elizabeth Morrison wound off a length of the self-striping yarn in order to make two entrelac panels with matching colors, making sure she began the entrelac panel on each hand at the same point in the yarn's repeat.

You can also manipulate repeats in other ways. For example, if you use up the last of a ball of yarn and you are in the middle of an orange stripe, when you pick up the next ball of yarn, it may begin at blue, a different place in the repeat. You can wind off the yarn until you get to the same orange stripe, and join the new ball at that point so that you don't switch colors abruptly, mid-row. This is one of those times when knowing yourself helps. Some of my knitting friends can be quite persnickety about keeping stripe or other patterns consistent, and regularly wind off sections of self-patterning yarn as they are working on a project in order to get matching socks or mittens or sleeves. I have other friends who don't really care, and just let the colors fall where they may.

TRANSLATING REPEATS FROM SOCKS TO OTHER PROJECTS

It sounds pretty elemental, but it behooves the knitter who is playing with sock yarns to remember that sock yarns are designed first and foremost to be knit into socks. So when clever sock yarn engineers figure out how to dye yarns that automatically create, say, a fair isle pattern, or provide an illustration of what a particular yarn's stripes will look like, they're assuming that the finished product will be an average-sized sock.

In this book, we're using sock yarns to knit just about everything under the sun *except* socks. It's helpful to keep in mind that as we use sock yarn to knit hats or vests or shawls, we may have to make some adaptations in order to get the best result possible.

In the previous sections, we spent a lot of time talking about the yarn's repeat, and how the repeat dictates what the finished knitting will look like. We saw how the repeat can create stripes or more complex patterns, and how it can cause some yarns to pool. We also saw how changing factors like the circumference of the sock or the rate at which the knitter is using yarn can affect the way the pattern looks in the finished sock. Remember that when you are using a sock yarn for another item, you are of necessity changing factors like circumference and the rate at which the yarn is taken up by the knitting. That can affect the way a sock yarn looks, sometimes drastically.

Consider the difference between knitting a sock and a rectangular scarf. The sock is knit as a tube in the round while the scarf is knit back-and-forth in a flat piece. The sock engineers created a yarn designed to work when knit in rounds—concentric circles sitting on top of each other. The pattern may not show up the same way if you're knitting back and forth, creating rows of knitting that alternate left-to-right and right-to-left, since the individual color segments of the yarn may end up stacking up in a different pattern.

Think, too, about the varying sizes of knitted items. While socks tend to hover around 7 to 8, maybe 9 inches/17.8 to 20.3, 22.9cm in circumference, you'll find greater size variations in other knitted items. A sweater front or back ranges from 18 to 20 inches/45.7 to 50.8cm in width to as many as 25 inches/63.5cm or more, depending on its size. An adult hat may be 20 inches/50.5cm in circumference, while a thin scarf may be only 4 or 5 inches/10.2 or 12.7cm in width. These varying widths or circumferences may affect the way a sock yarn looks when knit up. A pattern that pops when knit in an 8-inch/20.3cm tube may look splotchy and blah when spread out over a 24-inch/61cm flat sweater back. A hand-paint that doesn't pool when knit into a sock may create blotches of color when knit into a shawl. Stripes that are 1-inch/2.5cm thick when knit in a sock may be 2 or 3 inches/5.1 or 7.6cm thick if knit into a narrow scarf, or may end up only a ¼ inch/6mm thick when knit into a sweater piece. The pattern may even disappear entirely, turning into zigzags or single lines of each color, if the changes in size and knitting direction are significant.

What does this mean for you, the knitter? Well, it means that when you're using a sock yarn to knit something other than socks, you'll need to keep factors like knitting direction and width/circumference in the back of your mind. If you're using a self-patterning or hand-painted sock yarn for something knit flat or multidirectionally rather than in the round, keep an eye out for the way the pattern is stacking up to make sure you like the effect you're getting. Likewise, if you're knitting a piece that is significantly larger or smaller than 7 to 9 inches/17.8 to

Wrist warmers are roughly seven or eight inches in circumference, the same size as most socks. Thus, self-patterning sock yarns designed for socks tend to work well for them.

22.9cm in width or circumference, know that the effect you get from a self-patterning or self-striping yarn may be quite different from the picture on the label. Trial and error is going to play a large role here. You may quite like the effect you get, even if it's not exactly what the sock yarn engineers intended, or you may decide that this particular sock yarn isn't right for this project. Or you may end up having to manipulate the way you use the yarn to get an effect you like.

We've tried to take into account the tendencies of self-stripers and self-patterning yarns in designing the projects in this book. For example, it's not a coincidence that the Calico Scarf is seven inches wide: It was deliberately done to optimize the way the self-patterning yarn would knit up since that is about the same circumference a typical sock would be. And self-patterning yarn works beautifully in the Hodgepodge Wristers for the same reason: The circumference of the wristers closely approximates the circumference of an average-sized sock, allowing the yarn to perform as engineered.

Some things to keep in mind when you use self-patterning or hand-painted sock yarns for items other than socks:

- Compare the width of the item you're knitting with the circumference of a typical sock. If there's a big difference, you may end up with a different look than the picture on the label.

- Ditto for changes in knitting direction: When knitting in rows rather than in the round, or doing a multidirectional technique (say, entrelac), be prepared for a look that may differ from what you expected.

- Remember that any time you work increases or decreases, you are changing the width or circumference of your piece, and therefore the pattern created by the yarn may change. Decreases worked for the top of a hat may alter the pattern just at the top, where the decreases are worked. When a sleeve gets wider at the top, the pattern may change gradually as the increases start to add up to a change in width. Other potential trouble spots: binding off stitches for armhole, neckline or shoulder; shawls that rely on a gradual series of increases or decreases; fingers or thumbs that are significantly smaller than the hands of a mitten or glove; raglan or yoke shaping; and working neckbands or armbands. All of these spots involve changes in the size of the knitting, and therefore could change the way your hand-painted or self-patterning sock yarn looks when knit up.

- Changes in pattern stitch may also create changes in the yarn's effects. Ribbing uses up yarn faster and tends to draw in, thus a ribbed edging may look quite a bit different than the same number of stitches worked in stockinette.

- For results that look the most like the yarn's label, opt for an item or portion of the garment that is close to sock-sized in width or circumference (7 to 9 inches/17.8 to 22.9cm).

- Mixing a self-patterning yarn with a solid can disguise some of these effects. For example, if you're making a hat, use a solid yarn for a ribbed cuff, where the ribbing will alter the pattern, and use a self-striper for the rest of the hat.

- Self-stripers will be more forgiving than yarns with more complicated patterns, like jacquard or fair isle. Stripes are created by relatively long segments of color, while more intricate patterns involve short, alternating segments of color. It's easier to work with long unbroken stretches of color than to manipulate shorter segments of color that change frequently.

- If a hand-painted yarn is pooling in just one section of the project, try the tips on page 20 to see if you can minimize or eliminate the pooling effects. For example, if your yarn knits up beautifully in the beginning of your hat but starts to pool when you begin making decreases at the crown, start alternating miniballs once you begin the top decreases.

focused on fingering weight

THERE ARE SO MANY wonderful sock yarns today and I wanted to include as many kinds in this book as I could. At the same time, I was, obviously, limited to a certain number of projects and pages. One concession I made to keep the scope of the book manageable was to focus on fingering weight sock yarns—yarns that that knit about 7 to 9 stitches per inch (2.54cm) in stockinette stitch.

I chose to focus on fingering weight yarns for two reasons. First of all, fingering weight yarn is the most common weight of yarn used for socks—and with good reason. Socks need to be worn on the foot under a shoe. Really thick yarn makes really thick socks, which can make one's shoes pinch or even not fit at all. Thicker folds of fabric can create irritation and blisters. And thinner socks allow perspiration to dry faster (who wants to walk around all day in damp, sweaty socks?). If I had to limit my yarn choices at all, it made sense to stick with the most common weight of sock yarn.

But there's another key advantage to featuring patterns that are all knit in the same weight of yarn: yarn substitution. Most of the projects in this book feature Craft Yarn Council Category 1 yarns, which means that any other Category 1 yarn is a potential substitute. (You'll have to consider other factors

before substituting, like color, quantity, and drape, but you've got a big head start by narrowing your search to only Category 1/ fingering weight yarns.)

How Do I Know if My
Sock Yarn is the Right Weight?

Yarn substitution is an entire topic of its own, but suffice it to say that yarn comes in various thicknesses. Thick yarn makes thick fabric; thinner yarn makes thinner fabric. To get a project that looks like the one in the photo, and that is the same dimensions as listed in the pattern, you have to work with yarn that is about the same thickness as the yarn used in the pattern. To make the process of yarn substitution easier, knitters divide yarns into general categories based on their thickness. You can find these categories in a handy chart created by the Craft Yarn Council (CYC):

www.craftyarncouncil.com/weight.html

Fingering weight yarn falls into Category 1 (called "Super Fine") on the Craft Yarn Council Chart. The vast majority of yarns sold today specify which category in the CYC Chart they belong to. Look for the little skein with the number in the middle of it; most also include the words "Category 1" or "Super-fine" or some combination thereof. When buying yarn for the projects in this book, or selecting yarn from your stash, select only yarns that are labeled as Category 1 yarns.

What if you have yarn that predates the CYC Chart, doesn't include the category designation, or is written in a language you can't translate? Look for any or all of these indicators that your yarn is, indeed, Category 1 yarn:

1. Look for the description "fingering weight," "sock weight," or "jumperweight." In some cases you might also see the phrase "4-ply" or "baby" yarn. You might find these descriptive phrases in the name of the yarn: "Yolanda Yak's 4-ply Sock Yarn," or a helpful description underneath the name: "Knancy Knitter's Soopersoft Wool, a fingering weight yarn."

2. Find the specified or ideal gauge, another piece of information that is usually spelled out on the label. You are looking for a yarn that knits at approximately 7 to 9 stitches per inch/2.54cm in stockinette stitch. (You may see the numbers given as multiples of 4 inches: 28 to 36 sts = 4 inches/10cm in St st.) Row gauge is more variable, but will probably fall in the 10 to 14 rows = 1 inch/2.54cm or 40 to 56 rows = 4 inches/10cm range.

3. Compare the length of the yarn in the skein to the weight of the skein. Fingering weight yarn tends to have about the same number of yards or meters relative to a specific measure of weight:

> 50g skeins = 180-225 yards/165-206m
> 100g skeins = 375-450 yds/343-411m
> 3.5/4oz skeins = 375-450 yds/343-411m
> 1.75/2oz skeins = 180-225 yards/165-206m

4. Look at the knitting needle size that is suggested for the yarn. Typically, fingering weight yarns are knit on 2-3.25mm/U.S. size 0 to 3 needles (in stockinette stitch). If the ball band recommends that you start swatching on a needle in this size range, it's another sign you're likely using a Category 1 yarn.

on swatching

YOU MAY BE ASKING yourself, "Hey, since all the patterns in this book use the same weight of yarn, do I really need to swatch?"

The answer is yes. Even if you start out with the same weight of yarn as the one shown in the book, even if you used the very same brand, even the very same color of yarn as the one used in the sample, you may end up with a finished item that differs greatly in size from the finished dimensions listed in the book. Some knitters knit tightly and might end up with a project smaller than the one shown in the book, while others knit loosely and could find that their project is much larger. To be sure your item ends up the size you want, please check your gauge carefully and adjust your needle size until your gauge matches the gauge called for in the pattern. Use the specified needle sizes *as a starting point* for determining with which needles to start swatching but don't be hesitant to switch needle sizes until you reach the specified gauge.

Want an example of why gauge matters? If you made a cap using 100 sts and the pattern called for a gauge of 5 sts to an inch (2.54cm), you'd end up with a hat about 20 inches/50.8cm in circumference if you got the required gauge. That hat would be just the right size to fit an adult. But if you got only 1 fewer stitch per inch, and knit at a gauge of 4 sts to an inch, the hat would be a whopping 25 inches/63.5cm in circumference when you were done—big enough to fit a basketball. If you got only 1 more stitch per inch, knitting at 6 stitches per inch instead of the required 5, you would end up with a hat that was 16.5 inches/41.9cm in circumference. The hat would fit a toddler quite nicely, but would be far too small for most adults.

yarn substitution: go for it!

I'VE NOTICED THAT SOME knitters are very uncomfortable with making projects in a yarn that is not exactly the same as the yarn shown in the sample project. Part of this may be unfamiliarity with the process of yarn substitution; part of it may be due to inexperience; part of it may be feeling like there's not enough time to play around with yarn if it means raveling out knitting and trying over and over. I do get this. Yet I want to encourage the tentative knitters out there to be open-minded about yarn choices when making the projects in this book. If you've got some sock yarns in your stash that you'd like to use, or if there's a sock yarn out there that you've been dying to try, go for it! Here are some tips to make it work:

- Make sure you're starting with a Category 1/ fingering weight yarn. (See page 27 for more information on how to do this.)

- One way to ease into substitution is to stick with the same brand and type of yarn, but pick a different colorway. If the sample is knit in yellow, but yellow makes you look sallow, opt for the same brand and type of yarn, but in, say, blue or indigo.

- Another way to take some of the guesswork out of substitution is to pick a yarn that is similar in appearance to the one used in the sample. Start determining what general category of sock yarn it falls into—solid vs. multicolor vs. self-patterning. The easiest way to achieve an effect similar to the sample is to use a yarn that's similar to the one used in the sample.

- Remember the general rule-of-thumb: Either the yarn does the work or the knitter does the work. Yarns with a lot going on—lots of self-patterning or striping, wild color combinations—tend to look better knit in simpler patterns, so the yarn won't overshadow the stitchwork. Conversely, solids and nearly solids are the best choices for more complicated stitch patterns. The uniformity of the color keeps the focus on your stitchwork rather than the color changes of the yarn.

- Think about the characteristics of the fiber in the yarn you'd like to use and compare it with the fiber in the sample yarn. Fibers like silk, bamboo, tencel, and rayon have lots of drape and sheen. This makes them good substitutes for scarves and cowls (like the Lisatra Cowl).

Wool tends to be springy and elastic—good if you're doing more complicated stitch patterns like cables (think the Roselein Cap). Wool yarns are also excellent for stranded knitting, since the wool strands grab to each other to create a fabric without holes. For baby items, consider using a superwash fiber or blend to make Mom's job easier.

- Use the Yarn Symbols next to each pattern to help select yarn. We've given you some guidance as to the types of yarns that are particularly suited to each individual project.

- Ask for help at your friendly local yarn shop, or take your pattern or project to your knitting group and get its advice. Or use the internet to get ideas for yarn substitution. Searching a specific pattern on Ravelry or Googling it may turn up photographs of that pattern knit in various yarn choices.

- If you're not confident with yarn substitution, pick the right time to experiment. Don't stress yourself out trying to substitute yarns if you've got a deadline for your knitting (e.g., a baby gift that needs to be finished for a shower), if the project is particularly big or complicated, or at a time when you're already frantic from a busy week at work.

- Remember that part of the fun of knitting is creating your own unique project, unlike anyone else's. Even if you used the exact same pattern and the exact same yarn as a sample, your project will be uniquely yours simply because you made it.

One
SKEIN
PROJECTS

Lisatra Short Cowl

DESIGNER: Carol J. Sulcoski   SKILL LEVEL: Easy to Intermediate

Cowls are a wonderful way to show off an exquisite color of sock yarn while keeping its softness snuggled up against your face. This cowl uses a luscious silk/wool blend in a bright color which makes the mesh-like German lace pattern pop.

PATTERN STITCH

German Lace (multiple of 14 sts):

Rnd 1: *P1, yo, skp, k8, k2tog, yo, p1; rep from * to end.

Rnd 2: *P1, k1, yo, skp, k6, k2tog, yo, k1, p1; rep from * to end.

Rnd 3: *P1, k2, yo, skp, k4, k2tog, yo, k2, p1; rep from * to end.

Rnd 4: *P1, k3, yo, skp, k2, k2tog, yo, k3, p1; rep from * to end.

Rnd 5: *P1, k4, yo, skp, k2tog, yo, k4, p1; rep from * to end.

Rep Rnds 1-5 for pat.

FINISHED MEASUREMENTS

Circumference: 24"/61cm

Height: 9"/23cm

MATERIALS AND TOOLS

Black Bunny Fibers Softsilk Sock (50% merino wool, 50% silk; 3.5oz/100g = 425yd/389m): 1 skein, color Kristi's Fave—approx 200yd/183m of fingering weight yarn (**1**)

Knitting needles: 4.0mm (size 6 U.S.) 24" circular needle or size to obtain gauge

Stitch marker

Tapestry needle

GAUGE

22 sts/30 rows = 4"/10cm in German Lace

Always take time to check your gauge.

Chart

14	13	12	11	10	9	8	7	6	5	4	3	2	1	
−					O	/	\	O					−	5
−				O	/			\	O				−	4
−			O	/					\	O			−	3
−		O	/							\	O		−	2
−	O	/									\	O	−	1

Stitch Key

- □ knit
- O yarn over
- \ ssk
- / k2tog
- − purl

INSTRUCTIONS

CO 126 sts. PM and join for working in the rnd, being careful not to twist.

Knit 1 rnd.

Purl 1 rnd.

Rep these 2 rnds one more time.

Work in German Lace until cowl measures approx 8¾"/22cm from beg, ending with Rnd 5.

Knit 1 rnd.

Purl 1 rnd.

Rep these 2 rnds one more time.

BO.

FINISHING

Weave in ends. Block as desired.

Roselein Hat

DESIGNER: Franklin Habit   SKILL LEVEL: Intermediate

The crisp stitch definition of this hand-painted yarn is perfect for showing off the cables on Franklin Habit's delightful hat. A Chicago resident familiar with bitter winter winds, Habit cleverly includes earflaps for extra warmth—and extra style.

INSTRUCTIONS

Flaps (make 2):

Using Judy's Magic Cast On (see page 38), CO 8 sts onto each of 2 needles—16 sts.

Note: Flap will be worked in the rnd, keeping half of the sts on each needle at all times.

Knit 1 rnd.

Work flap pat from Chart A. Work Rows 1–16, then rep Rows 9–16 three times for a total of 40 rows from chart—56 sts.

Turn work inside out (do not remove from needles), and weave in tail from CO on WS. Turn work RS out.

To close flap, arrange needles so that left tips (28 sts each) are in the left hand, parallel, with working yarn coming from the first st on the back needle. With right tip of front needle, knit together first st on front needle and first st on back needle. Rep across all live sts, knitting next st on front needle together with its

FINISHED MEASUREMENTS

Circumference at Brim: 21"/53cm

Brim to Crown: 8"/20cm

Lower End of Flaps to Crown: 12"/30cm

MATERIALS AND TOOLS

Blue Moon Fiber Arts Socks That Rock® Mediumweight (100% superwash merino; 5.5oz/155g = 380yd/347m): 1 skein, color "True Blood" red—approx. 300yd/274m of sport weight yarn (2)

Knitting needles: Two 3.25mm (size 3 U.S.) 24" circular needles or size needed to obtain gauge

Stitch marker

Cable needle

Tapestry needle

2 buttons, 1"/25mm diameter

GAUGE

24 sts/38 ½ rows = 4 ½"/10cm in St st

Always take time to check your gauge.

SPECIAL ABBREVIATIONS

M1: With tip of RH needle, pick up running thread to right of next st on LH needle and place over tip of LH needle. Knit into back of loop formed by running thread.

What is Judy's Magic Cast-On?

Franklin Habit's stunning cap pattern begins by telling the knitter to cast on stitches "using Judy's Magic Cast-On." If you aren't familiar with Judy Becker and her ingenious method of casting on stitches, you're in for a treat. Frustrated with existing methods for beginning toe-up socks, Becker developed her own way to invisibly cast on stitches in two parallel rows. You can find complete instructions and photos online (http://knitty.com/ISSUEspring06/FEATmagiccaston.html) or in Becker's book, *Beyond Toes* (Indigo Frog Press, 2011).

counterpart on back needle, until you have a single row of 28 live sts on one needle.

*Purl 1 row, knit 1 row; rep from * until upper (plain, single-layered) portion of flap measures 1"/3cm.

BO.

To make button loop, CO 2 sts, leaving 6"/15cm tail. Work 2-stitch I-cord for 3"/8cm. BO. Cut yarn, leaving a 6"/15cm tail. Using tails at CO and BO, firmly sew cord ends to tip of flap to create a loop.

Head:

On one needle, CO 176 sts. PM and join for working in the rnd, being careful not to twist.

Knit 1 rnd.

Work Chart B 2 times. Note: Rep Chart B 22 times in each rnd.

Next rnd: [K2, ssk, k2tog, k2] around—132 sts.

Knit 1 rnd.

Next rnd: [K10, k2tog] around—121 sts.

Work, knitting all sts, until piece measures 7"/18cm from CO edge.

Next rnd: K2tog, knit to end of rnd—120 sts.

Remove beg of rnd marker. K60 sts. Knit rem 60 sts onto second needle. Rem of hat is worked with half of the sts on each needle at all times.

Rnd 1: [K2tog, k26, ssk] 4 times—112 sts.

Rnd 2: Knit.

Rnd 3: [K2tog, k24, ssk] 4 times—104 sts.

Rnd 4: Knit.

Continue to dec in this fashion, until 80 sts rem.

Knit 1 rnd.

Work Chart C (Crown)—8 sts. Note: Rep Chart C 2 times across each needle.

Cut working yarn, leaving 6"/15cm tail. Thread end of tail through tapestry needle and run tail through all live sts. Pull to close crown opening. Run yarn to WS of fabric and weave in.

FINISHING

Weave in ends on flaps and head. Soak and gently block all pieces.

With WS (purl) of upper flap facing WS of head, sew flaps to head at brim edge, approximately 7"/18cm apart.

Sew one button to the outside tip of each flap.

Chart A

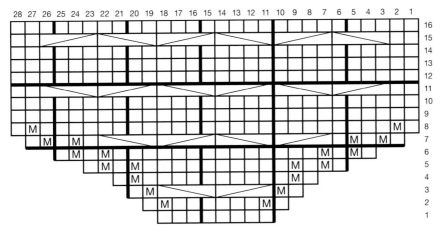

28 27 26 25 24 23 22 21 20 19 18 17 16 15 14 13 12 11 10 9 8 7 6 5 4 3 2 1

16 15 14 13 12 11 10 9 8 7 6 5 4 3 2 1

Chart B

8 7 6 5 4 3 2 1

8 7 6 5 4 3 2 1

Chart C

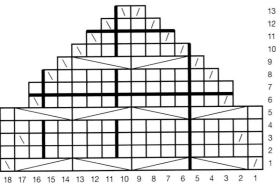

13 12 11 10 9 8 7 6 5 4 3 2 1

18 17 16 15 14 13 12 11 10 9 8 7 6 5 4 3 2 1

Stitch Key

☐ knit

M make one

\ ssk

/ k2tog

⬛ right cross

⬛ left cross

Calico Scarf

DESIGNER: Carol J. Sulcoski   SKILL LEVEL: Easy

Although this pattern couldn't be simpler, it yields a deceivingly complex result. Knitting the appropriate size rectangle showcases the clever self-patterning design of this sock yarn. A fabric back is then sewn directly to the knitted rectangle using a sewing machine. This scarf served as my travel project for several months, providing easy knitting in the car, at a baseball game, at friends' houses, and at the beach.

INSTRUCTIONS

CO 35 sts.

Beg with a RS row, work in St st until scarf measures 44"/112cm or desired length, ending with a WS row.

BO all sts knitwise.

Weave in ends and block as desired.

FINISHING

Cut two pieces of fabric, 9"/23cm by width of fabric. Using sewing machine, stitch these pieces together across their short edges, with RS facing each other. Iron open seam so seam lies flat.

FINISHED MEASUREMENTS

Length: 44"/112cm

Width: 9"/23cm

(before sewing on backing fabric)

MATERIALS AND TOOLS

Opal Hundertwasser 2 (75% superwash wool, 25% polyamide; 3 ½ oz/100g = 465yd/425m): 1 skein, color Der Weg von dir su mir zurück #823—approx 400yd/366m of fingering weight yarn (**1**)

½ yd/0.5m Timeless Treasures Happy Together Corduroy, 100% cotton, color Wildflower Bouquet in Cocoa #CCD8447—approx ½ yd/0.5m cotton fabric (approx 40–42"/ 102–107cm wide)

Knitting needles: 3.25mm (size 3 U.S.) needles or size to obtain gauge

Tapestry needle

Sewing thread, pins, and sewing needle

GAUGE

28 sts/36 rows = 4"/10cm in St st

Always take time to check your gauge.

Note: Quilting fabrics are typically sold in widths of 40–42"/102–107cm after the selvedge is removed. If your knitted piece is longer than that, you will have to sew two 9"/23cm pieces together to get sufficient length for your scarf backing. I chose to cut two 9"/23cm pieces the width of the fabric and sew them together so that I could place the fabric seam in the center of the scarf, where it will fall at the back of the neck when the scarf is worn. You can, of course, use one 40–42"/102–107cm width of fabric plus a smaller width for your scarf if you don't mind seeing the fabric seam near one end of the finished scarf.

Place knitted rectangle RS up on table, then place fabric on top of knitted rectangle with the WS of the fabric facing out (RS of knitted rectangle and fabric will be together). Sewn seam on fabric should fall at halfway point of knitted rectangle so that it will be hidden by back of neck when scarf is worn. Trim off excess fabric at ends, so that fabric is even with knitted edges. Pin around edges, leaving approximately 6"/15cm of scarf open at bottom center, near seam. Use sewing machine to carefully stitch where pins are, then remove pins. Turn scarf right-side out and hand-sew 6"/15cm opening.

Fortunate Cowl

DESIGNER: Melissa Morgan-Oakes   **SKILL LEVEL:** Intermediate

You may not be able to take your dog with you wherever you go, but if you're lucky, you can get a skein of sock yarn custom-dyed to match your dog's fur. Then you can knit it into a cowl as soft and snuggly as the dog himself.

FINISHED MEASUREMENTS
Circumference 16 ½"/42cm

Width 6 ¾"/17cm

MATERIALS AND TOOLS
Valley Yarns Charlemont (60% fine superwash merino wool/20% mulberry silk/20% polyamide; 3.5oz/100g = 439yds/401m): 1 skein, color Yoshi—approx 430yds/401m of fingering weight yarn

Note: Color Yoshi is available at the Webs store.

Knitting needles: 3.75mm (size 5 U.S.) 18" circular needle or size to obtain gauge

Stitch markers

Cable needle

Tapestry needle

GAUGE
26 sts/32 rnds = 3"/7.5cm in charted pattern stitch, unstretched

PATTERN STITCH

Seed Stitch (multiple of 2 sts):

Rnd 1: *K1, p1; rep from * to end of rnd.

Rnd 2: *P1, k1; rep from * to end of rnd.

Rep Rnds 1 and 2 for pat.

Chart

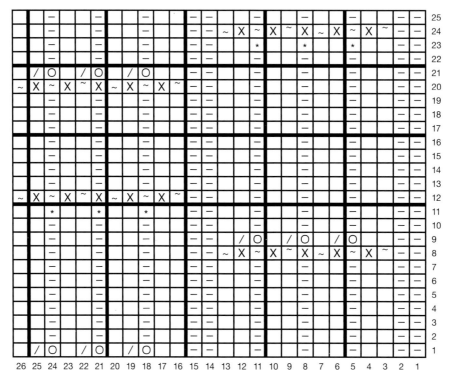

Stitch Key

☐ knit

○ yarn over

− purl

╱ k2tog

~X~X~X~X~X~ slip 6 stitches to cable needle, hold in back, k2, p1, k2 next 5 stitches, then p1, k2, p1, k2 from cable needle

* drop stitch from needle to make run, then make yarn over to replace dropped stitch

INSTRUCTIONS

CO 130 sts using long-tail cast-on. PM and join for working in the rnd, being careful not to twist.

Work in Seed St for 3 rnds.

Note: First round of charted pattern is a set-up round. Do this round only once, at the beginning of the pattern. Do not repeat this round on subsequent repeats of the pattern.

Change to charted pattern.

Work Rnd 1 of chart only once, working 5 repeats of the pattern around the perimeter of the cowl.

Work Rnds 2–25 of chart.

Rep Rnds 2–25 of chart one more time.

Work Rnds 2–13 of chart one time.

Cowl should measure approx 6 ½"/16.5cm long.

Work 3 rnds of Seed St.

BO purlwise.

FINISHING

Release all of the dropped stitches using your fingers. Weave in ends. Soak the cowl in cool water and a no-rinse wool-safe wash for about 20 minutes. Remove the cowl from the water and squeeze out excess moisture. Lay flat to dry.

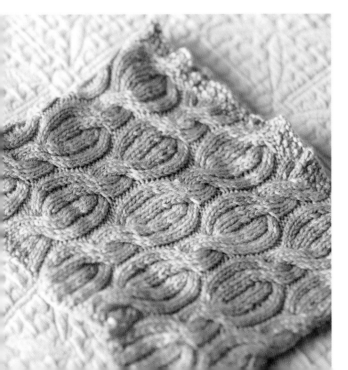

Compostela Scarf

DESIGNER: Carol J. Sulcoski   SKILL LEVEL: Easy

I have always been fascinated with yarns that slowly blend from one color into the next. This scarf was designed with these yarns in mind: See how the gentle curves of the lace pattern echo the yarn's color changes. But the pattern is versatile enough to work well with other types of sock yarns, too, as you can see by the solid-colored version. A good blocking really helps to make the lace pattern pop.

PATTERN STITCH

Ripple Lace:

Rows 1, 3 and 5 (RS): K1, *k2tog, k2, kfb, k1, kfb, k2, k2tog tbl; rep from * to end.

Rows 2, 4, 6, 7, 8, 12, and 13: K1, purl to last st, k1.

Row 9: Knit.

Row 10: K1, *yo, p2tog; rep from * to last st, k1.

Row 11: K1, *k1 tbl, k1; rep from * to last st, k1.

Row 14: K1, purl to last st, k1.

Rep Rows 1–14 for pat.

FINISHED MEASUREMENTS

Version 1: 82"/208cm long x 7"/18cm wide

Version 2: 76"/193cm long x 6½"/17cm wide

MATERIALS AND TOOLS

Version 1: Universal Yarns Poems Sock (75% superwash wool, 25% nylon; 3.5oz/100g = 459yd/ 420m): 1 skein, color Cold Fire #957—approx 425yd/389m of fingering weight yarn **(1)**

Version 2: Quince & Co. Tern (75% American wool, 25% silk; 1.75oz/50g = 221yd/202m): 2 skeins, color Wampum #147—approx 400yd/365m of fingering weight yarn **(1)**

Knitting needles: 3.5mm (size 4 U.S.) needles or size to obtain gauge

Stitch holder or spare double pointed needle

Tapestry needle

GAUGE

24 sts/44 rows = 5"/24cm in Ripple Lace using Version 1 yarn, after blocking
22 sts/30 rows = 4¼"/10cm in Ripple Lace using Version 2 yarn, after blocking

Always take time to check your gauge.

SPECIAL ABBREVIATION

Kfb: Knit in the front and back of the same stitch—1 st increased.

INSTRUCTIONS

Note: You will knit the scarf in two identical pieces, each working from end to center; then you will graft the pieces together at the center.

First Section:

CO 34 sts.

*Knit 6 rows.

Work 6 reps of Ripple Lace.

Rep from * 3 more times for Version 1 and only 2 more times for Version 2.

Knit 6 rows.

Cut yarn. Leave live sts on a holder or spare needle.

Second Section:

Using remainder of yarn (or second skein), make second half of scarf to match, but do not cut yarn after you knit the last 6 rows.

FINISHING

Holding both pieces with RS facing you, graft live sts together using Kitchener st. Weave in ends and block.

Deux Violettes Gloves

DESIGNER: Ruth Garcia-Alcantud   SKILL LEVEL: Intermediate

A twist on a classic, these long gloves are a must for the autumn and winter seasons. With a reverse Stockinette stitch cuff and some knockout buttons, these gloves add high style without bulk, due to the lightweight fabric created by this gorgeous sock yarn.

INSTRUCTIONS

Cuff:

Beg at lower edge of cuff, CO 72 sts. Work back and forth in rows.

Beg with a knit row, work in St st for 2 rows.

Next (dec) row (RS): K2, ssk, knit to last 4 sts, k2tog, K2—70 sts.

Rep dec row every RS row 6 times more then every 4th row 4 times—50 sts.

Work even, if necessary, until piece measures 3"/8cm from beg, ending with a RS row. BO.

CO 3 sts onto one dpn. With RS facing and starting at last BO st, *pick up and knit 1 st from edge of piece—4 sts. Work I-cord edging as follows:

Next row: K2, ssk. Move sts to other end of needle. Rep from * across both side edges and CO edge. BO. Do not work I-cord across BO edge of cuff.

FINISHED MEASUREMENTS
To fit 6"/15cm wrist, 7 ¼"/18cm hand circumference at base of fingers

MATERIALS AND TOOLS
Classic Elite Alpaca Sox (60% alpaca, 20% merino wool, 20% nylon; 3.5oz/100g = 450yd/411m): 1 skein, color Byzantine purple #1895—approx 275yd/251m of fingering weight yarn (1)

Knitting needles: 2.75mm (size 2 U.S.) 24" circular needle or size to obtain gauge

3.25mm (size 3 U.S.) double pointed needles

Stitch markers

Waste yarn and crochet hook (for provisional cast on)

Tapestry needle

Stitch holder

16 buttons, ¼"/6mm diameter

Sewing thread in matching shade

Sewing needle

GAUGE
32 sts/40 rows = 4"/10cm in St st

Always take time to check your gauge.

Lower Hand:

With WS (knit) of cuff facing, pick up and purl 48 sts across BO edge, PM after the 23rd and 25th sts. Join for working in the rnd.

Work in St st for 2 rnds.

Next (inc) rnd: Knit to marker, sl marker, M1, knit to marker, M1, sl marker, knit to end—50 sts.

Rep inc rnd every 2nd rnd 9 times and every 4th rnd once—70 sts.

Continue until piece measures 3"/7.5cm from base of pick up edge.

With waste yarn and crochet hook, chain 12 sts. Set aside.

Upper Hand:

Next rnd: K23, sl next 24 sts to holder; with crochet chain, pick up and k8 sts from center sts of chain, knit rem 23 sts from hand—54 sts rem.

Next (dec) rnd: Knit to marker, sl marker, ssk, knit to 2 sts before next marker, k2tog, sl marker, knit to end—52 sts.

Rep this dec rnd every 4th rnd once—50 sts.

Work even until hand measures 5"/13cm from base of pick-up edge.

Pinky:

K6, CO 4 sts using the Thumb Method, leave foll 38 sts on holder, k6 from opposite side of hand—16 sts. Join for working in the rnd.

Work in St st until pinky measures 2"/5cm.

Next (dec) rnd: *K2tog, k2; rep from * to end—12 sts.

Next (dec) rnd: *K2tog; rep from * to end—6 sts.

Cut yarn, leaving a 5"/13cm tail. Thread yarn on tapestry needle, weave needle through rem sts, cinch tight and secure end.

Ring Finger:

Pick up 4 sts from CO at side of pinky, pick up and k5 sts from holder, CO 4 sts using the Thumb Method, pick up and k5 sts from opposite side of hand—18 sts. Join for working in the rnd.

Work in St st until finger measures 2 ½"/6cm.

Next (dec) rnd: K2, *k2tog, K2; rep from * to end—14 sts.

Next (dec) rnd: *K2tog; rep from * to end—7 sts.

Cut yarn, leaving a 5"/13cm tail. Thread yarn on tapestry needle, weave needle through rem sts, cinch tight and secure end.

Middle Finger:

Pick up 4 sts from CO at side of ring finger, pick up and k6 sts from holder, CO 4 sts using the Thumb Method, pick up and k6 sts from opposite side of hand—20 sts. Join for working in the rnd.

Work in St st until finger measure 3"/8cm.

Next (dec) rnd: *K2tog, K2; rep from * to end—15 sts.

Next (dec) rnd: K1, *k2tog; rep from * to end—8 sts.

Cut yarn, leaving a 5"/13cm tail. Thread yarn on tapestry needle, weave needle through rem sts, cinch tight and secure end.

Index Finger:

Pick up 4 sts from CO at side of middle finger, pick up and k8 sts from holder, pick up and k8 sts from opposite side of hand—20 sts. Join for working in the rnd.

Work in St st until finger measures 2 ¾"/7 cm.

Next (dec) rnd: *K2tog, K2; rep from * to end—15 sts.

Next (dec) rnd: K1, *k2tog; rep from * to end— 8 sts.

Cut yarn, leaving a 5"/13cm tail. Thread yarn on tapestry needle, weave needle through rem sts, cinch tight and secure end.

Thumb:

Carefully unpick the provisional CO chain, knitting the 8 sts as you go. Work 1 st from held sts, PM, work 22 sts from held sts, PM, work last held st—32 sts. Join for working in the rnd.

Next (dec) rnd: Knit to 2 sts before marker, k2tog, sl marker, knit to marker, sl marker, ssk.

Rep this dec rnd every 2nd rnd 4 times—22 sts.

Work even until thumb measures 2"/5cm.

Next (dec) rnd: K2, *k2tog, k2; rep from * to end—17 sts.

Next (dec) rnd: K1, *k2tog; rep from * to end—9 sts.

Cut yarn, leaving a 5"/13cm tail. Thread yarn on tapestry needle, weave needle through rem sts, cinch tight and secure end.

FINISHING

Weave in ends, paying special attention to the join areas on fingers. With sewing thread and needle, sew buttons on edge of cuffs (as shown in photograph), going through both sides of cuff. Sew 4 pairs (8 buttons) on each glove. Fasten off thread securely.

Vert Lace Cap

DESIGNER: Hunter Hammersen   SKILL LEVEL: Intermediate

This lovely lace hat is a perfect pattern when you want to play with lace but don't want to take on a big project. It works up quickly, and the finished hat is quite stretchy, making it perfect for gift knitting.

INSTRUCTIONS

CO 70 (84, 98, 112) sts. PM and join for working in the rnd, being careful not to twist.

Cuff:

Work the Cuff Chart once.

Body:

Work the Main Chart until cap reaches desired height before shaping crown, end with Rnd 10 of Main Chart.

Shape Crown:

Work the Decrease Chart once. Draw yarn through the 5 (6, 7, 8) rem sts and pull to close opening.

FINISHING

Weave in ends. Block. Note: The lace pat is best seen after a vigorous blocking.

FINISHED MEASUREMENTS

Circumference at Brim: 15 (18, 21, 24)"/38 (46, 53, 61)cm

MATERIALS AND TOOLS

Spud & Chloë Fine (80% wool, 20% silk; 2.25oz/65g = 248yd/227m): 1 skein, color Cricket #7804—approx 150yd/137m of fingering weight yarn (1)

Knitting needles: 2.75mm (size 2 U.S.) double pointed needles or circular needle or size needed to obtain gauge

Stitch marker

GAUGE

14 sts = 3"/8cm in Cuff Chart, after blocking. The lace grows considerably after blocking, so it is important to measure on a blocked swatch.

Always take time to check your gauge.

Blocking a Cap

Blocking a flat piece of lace is one thing (see page 58), but how do you block a hat that's knit in the round? If you happen to have access to a Styrofoam form, like the ones used to hold wigs, you can stretch your hat over the form and pin it into place. Admittedly, not everyone has a foam head lying around the garage, so in that case, you'll have to be inventive. Try finding a kitchen bowl with a circumference that is similar to your desired finished hat circumference. (I blocked the delightful cap you see here in just this way the night before our photo shoot. I was very lucky I found just the right sized bowl!) Other options include an inflated balloon (although pinning is then out-of-the-question), or hand towels wadded into the desired shape. Although blocking is essential for most lace items, you'll find that the Vert Lace Cap particularly shines after it's been blocked.

Cuff Chart

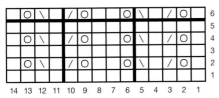

Main Chart

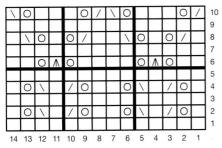

Stitch Key

□ knit

○ yarn over

\ ssk

/ k2tog

⋀ centered double decrease

■ no stitch

Decrease Chart

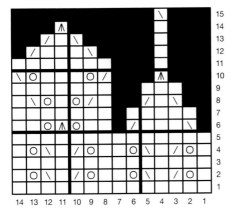

Habitude Lace Scarf

DESIGNER: Brooke Nico **SKILL LEVEL:** Intermediate

Inspired by men who love holes in their knitting, this scarf features a lace pattern that is manly (but women like it, too). The argyle-shaped eyelets make this an excellent choice for wearing with a kilt or wool coat. A variation on the pattern stitch adds nupps for those seeking a more embellished look.

INSTRUCTIONS:

CO 53 sts.

Purl 1 wrong side row.

Work Rows 1–48 of chart. Only right side rows are charted, all wrong side rows are purl across. For men's scarf, work nupp stitches as knit sts. Rep chart a total of 11 times.

BO loosely after last rep.

FINISHING

Weave in ends and block.

FINISHED MEASUREMENTS

Length: 60"/152cm

Width: 8"/20cm

MATERIALS AND TOOLS

Swan's Island Fingering Weight Organic Yarn (100% organic merino wool; 3.5oz/100g = 525yd/480m): 1 skein, color Teal—approx 400yd/366m of fingering weight yarn (1)

Swatch shown in color Rose Quartz

Knitting needles: 3.5mm (size 4 U.S.) needles, or size to obtain gauge

Scissors

GAUGE

26 sts/ 36 rows = 4"/10cm in pat, after blocking

Always take time to check your gauge.

SPECIAL ABBREVIATION

Make Nupp: Into the next stitch work [k1, (yo, yo, k1) 3 times], drop stitch off left needle (10 loops made out of 1 stitch). On the return row, when you come to these stitches, slip them one at a time to the right needle, dropping extra wraps (7 stitches slipped), slip 7 stitches back to left needle, and p7tog.

Blocking Your Lace

When you finally bind off the last stitch of a lace project, like Brooke Nico's wonderful Habitude Scarf, you may be a bit dismayed at the way your project looks. Where are the delicate loops and swirls that you so carefully knit in? Why does it scrunch together like that, lying in a sad little heap? Rest assured that there likely isn't anything wrong with your lace; it just needs a good blocking.

Because knitted lace involves a lot of stitch manipulation—yarnovers, decreases, nupps—the fabric you've created won't lay flat when it's fresh off the needles. You need to coax it into shape by blocking it. Begin by weaving in any loose ends—but don't cut the tails off. (Better to cut off the tails after the stretching is over, so the tails don't pop out.) Next, soak the scarf in lukewarm water, with a teeny bit of a rinse-free wool wash like Eucalan or Soak. Let the scarf have a good long soak, until it's saturated. Drain the water and gently transfer the scarf to an absorbent bath towel. Roll it in the towel until most of the excess water is gone. Next is the most important part: Lay the scarf out on your blocking surface and use rustproof pins to hold out the corners. Continue to add pins, gently coaxing and stretching the lace into shape. (Many lace knitters use blocking wires, threaded through the edges of each side, instead of pins.) Let the scarf dry thoroughly, unpin, and voilá! Gorgeous lace.

Chart

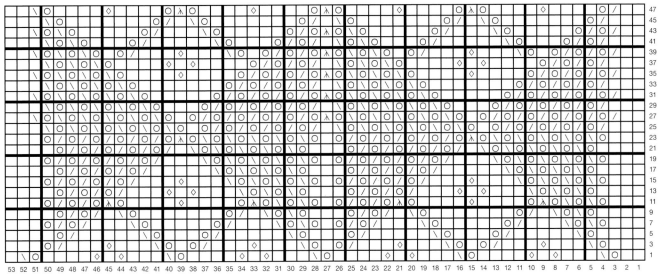

Stitch Key

This swatch was
knit with nupps.

□   knit on RS, purl on WS

O   yarn over

\   ssk

/   k2tog

λ   slip 1, k2tog, psso

◇   make nupp (for scarf
shown on page 56, work
plain knit st instead)

Golden Lace Baby Cardigan

DESIGNER: Erika Flory   SKILL LEVEL: Intermediate

Sock yarn is a great choice for baby items: It's soft, comes in lovely colors, like this buttery-yellow hand-paint, and is often machine-washable. This dropped-shoulder vest features an easy lace border and classic seed stitch. It layers beautifully over that special party dress or more casual ensemble.

SEED STITCH:

On Back:

Row 1 (RS): [K1, p1] 2 (3, 4) times, knit to last 6 sts, [p1, k1] 2 (3, 4) times.Row 2: [P1, k1] 2 (3, 4) times, purl to last 6 sts, [k1, p1] 2 (3, 4) times.

Rep Rows 1 and 2 for pat.

INSTRUCTIONS

Back:

CO 64 (68, 72) sts.

Keeping first and last 4 (1, 3) sts in St st, work Lace Edging for 10 rows.

Change to St st and work even until piece measures 4 ½ (5, 5 ½)"/11 (13, 14)cm from cast-on edge (measure from bottom point of lace).

Keeping first and last 4 (6, 8) sts in Seed St, work even in St st until piece measures 8 ½ (9, 9 ½)"/22 (23, 24) cm from cast-on edge, ending with a WS row.

FINISHED MEASUREMENTS

Chest (buttoned): 20 ½ (21 ¾, 23)"/52 (55, 58)cm

Back length from shoulder: 9 (9 ½, 10)"/23 (24, 25)cm

MATERIALS AND TOOLS

Malabrigo Sock (100% superwash merino wool; 3.5oz/100g = 440yd/400m): 1 skein, color ochre #803—approx 440yd/400m of fingering weight yarn **(1)**

Knitting needles: 3.5mm (size 4 U.S.) or size to obtain gauge

Stitch marker

Tapestry needle

3 buttons, ⅜"/10mm

GAUGE

25 sts/36 rows = 4"/10cm in St st

Always take time to check your gauge.

PATTERN STITCH

Lace Edging (multiple of 11 sts):

Row 1 (RS): *Ssk, k3, yo, k1, yo, k3, k2tog; rep from * to end.

Rows 2, 4, 6 and 8 (WS): Purl.

Row 3: *Ssk, k2, yo, k1, yo, ssk, yo, k2, k2tog; rep from * to end.

Row 5: *Ssk, k1, yo, k1, (yo, ssk) 2 times, yo, k1, k2tog; rep from * to end.

Row 7: *Ssk, yo, k1, (yo, ssk) 3 times, yo, k2tog; rep from * to end.

Row 9: *K1, p1, k7, p1, k1; rep from * to end.

Row 10: *P1, k1, p7, k1, p1; rep from * to end.

SHAPE SHOULDERS:

Working in St st, BO 6 (7, 7) sts at beg of next 4 rows, then BO 6 (6, 7) sts at beg of next 2 rows.

BO rem 28 (28, 30) sts for back neck. PM at center of back neck.

left front

CO 37 (40, 42) sts.

Row 1 (RS): K0 (1, 1), work odd rows of Lace Edging to last 4 (6, 8) sts, [p1, k1] 2 (3, 4) times.

Row 2 (WS): [P1, k1] 2 (3, 4) times, work even rows of Lace Edging to last 0 (1, 1) sts, p0 (1, 1).

Rep these 2 rows 4 more times for Lace Edging (for a total of 10 rows).

Work in St st, keeping 4 (6, 8) front edge sts in Seed St as established, until piece measures 4½ (5, 5½)"/10 (11, 14)cm from cast-on edge, ending with a WS row.

SHAPE NECK EDGE:

Next (dec) row (RS): [K1, p1] 2 (3, 4) times, knit to last 8 sts, k2tog, [p1, k1] 3 times—36 (39, 41) sts.

Next row (WS): [P1, k1] 3 times, purl to last 4 (6, 8) sts, [k1, p1] 2 (3, 4) times.

Rep dec row every other row 7 (8, 8) more times, then every 4th row 5 times—24 (26, 28) sts rem.

Work even, if necessary, until piece measures 8½ (9, 9½)"/22 (23, 24)cm from cast-on edge, ending with a WS row.

SHAPE SHOULDER:

BO 6 (7, 8) sts at beg of next 2 RS rows, then BO 6 sts at beg of next RS row—6 sts rem for left neck band. Continue in Seed St on rem 6 sts until band measures 2 (2¼, 2½)"/5 (6, 6)cm from shoulder. BO.

Mark for buttons at ½"/1cm, 2"/5cm and 3½"/9cm from bottom of button band.

right front

CO 37 (40, 42) sts.

Row 1 (RS): [K1, p1] 2 (3, 4) times, work odd rows of Lace Edging to last 0 (1, 1) sts, k0 (1, 1).

Row 2 (WS): P0 (1, 1), work even rows of Lace Edging to last 4 (6, 8) sts, [p1, k1] 2 (3, 4) times.

Rep these 2 rows 4 more times for Lace Edging and at the same time work buttonhole on RS at ½"/1cm from cast-on edge as follows: K1, p1, k2tog, yo, [k1, p1] 0 (1, 2) times.

Work in St st, keeping 4 (6, 8) sts in Seed St as established, until piece measures 4½ (5, 5½)"/10 (11, 14)cm from cast on edge, and at the same time work buttonholes on RS at 2"/5cm and 3½"/9cm from cast-on edge (opposite markers on left front), ending with a WS row.

SHAPE NECK EDGE:

Next (dec) row (RS): [K1, p1] 3 times, ssk, knit to last 4 (6, 8) sts, [p1, k1] 2 (3, 4) times—36 (39, 41) sts.

Next row (WS): [K1, p1] 2 (3, 4) times, purl to last 6 sts, [p1, k1] 3 times.

Rep dec row every other row 7 (8, 8) more times, then every 4th row 5 times—24 (26, 28) sts rem.

Work even, if necessary, until piece measures 8½ (9, 9½)"/22 (23, 24)cm from cast-on edge, ending with a RS row.

SHAPE SHOULDER:

BO 6 (7, 8) sts at beg next 2 WS rows, then BO 6 sts at beg next WS row—6 sts rem for right neckband. Continue in Seed St on rem 6 sts until band measures 2 (2¼, 2½)"/5 (6, 6)cm from shoulder. BO.

FINISHING

Block pieces to finished measurements.

Sew shoulders seams. Sew side seams from cast-on edge to beg of Seed St. Sew edges of neckbands together, then sew to back neck, matching center seam of neckband to marker at center back neck.

Weave in ends.

Sew buttons to left button band, opposite buttonholes.

Schematics

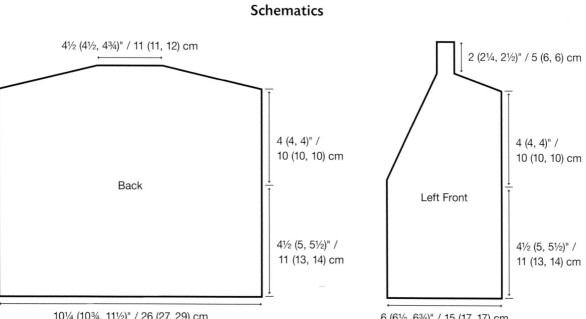

4½ (4½, 4¾)" / 11 (11, 12) cm

Back

4 (4, 4)" / 10 (10, 10) cm

4½ (5, 5½)" / 11 (13, 14) cm

10¼ (10¾, 11½)" / 26 (27, 29) cm

2 (2¼, 2½)" / 5 (6, 6) cm

Left Front

4 (4, 4)" / 10 (10, 10) cm

4½ (5, 5½)" / 11 (13, 14) cm

6 (6½, 6¾)" / 15 (17, 17) cm

Lace Edging Chart

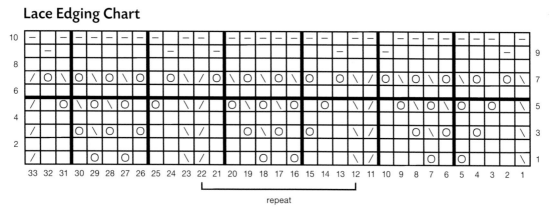

repeat

Stitch Key

☐   knit on RS, purl on WS

○   yarn over

\   ssk

/   k2tog

−   purl on RS, knit on WS

Poppy Beret

DESIGNER: Carol J. Sulcoski SKILL LEVEL: Easy

Lightweight sock yarn is perfect for this stylish beret: Made of superwash wool, it will keep you warm without crushing your hair. The crossed-stitch pattern is great for hand-painted yarns, as the movement of the stitches helps shuffle the yarn's color segments around, minimizing pooling and splotching.

INSTRUCTIONS

With smaller circular needle, CO 120 (132, 144) sts. PM and join for working in the rnd, being careful not to twist.

Brim:

Ribbing rnd: *K2, p2; rep from * to end.

Rep this rnd until brim measures 1 (1¼, 1¼)"/3 (3, 3) cm from beg.

Change to larger circular needle.

Next rnd: Knit.

Next (inc) rnd: *K1, kfb; rep to end of rnd—180 (198, 216) sts.

Beg working in Crossed Stitch and cont until piece measures 6¼ (7, 7¾)"/16 (18, 20)cm from beg, ending with Rnd 8.

FINISHED MEASUREMENTS

Brim circumference: Approx. 17 (19, 20½)"/43 (48, 52)cm

MATERIALS AND TOOLS

Wollmeise 100% Merino Superwash (100% superwash merino; 5.25oz/150g = 574yd/525m): 1 skein, color Rosenrot—approx 400yd/366m of fingering weight yarn (1)

Knitting needles: 2.75mm (size 2 U.S.) 16" circular needle or size to obtain gauge

2.75mm (size 2 U.S.) double pointed needles or second circular needle

2.25mm (size 1 U.S.) 16" circular needle or one size smaller than above

Stitch marker

Tapestry needle

GAUGE

28 sts/40 rnds = 4"/10cm in ribbing, slightly stretched, using smaller needles

30sts/36 rnds = 4"/10cm in Crossed Stitch using larger needles

PATTERN STITCH

Crossed Stitch (multiple of 6 sts):
Rnds 1 and 2: Knit.

Rnd 3: *P3, k3; rep from * to end.

Rnd 4: *P1, k1 into knit st below the next purl st, p1, k3; rep from * to end.

Rnds 5 and 6: Knit.

Rnd 7: *K3, p3; rep from * to end.

Rnd 8: *K3, p1, k1 into knit st below the next purl st, p1; rep from * to end.

Rep Rnds 1-8 for pat.

Beg decreases for crown:

Rnd 1: Knit.

Rnd 2: *Ssk, k2, k2tog; rep from * to end—120 (132, 144) sts.

Rnds 3 and 4: Work Rnds 3 and 4 of Crossed Stitch.

Rnd 5: Knit.

Rnd 6: *Ssk, k2, k2tog; rep from * to end—80 (88, 96) sts.

Rnd 7:

For smallest size only: K2, k2tog, p3, *k3, p3; rep from * to last 7 sts, k2, k2tog, p3—78 sts.

For middle size only: Ssk, k1, k2tog, p3, *k3, p3; rep from * to last 8 sts, k3, p2tog tbl, p1, p2tog—84 sts.

For largest size only: *K3, p3; rep from * to end.

Rnd 8: Work Rnd 8 of Crossed Stitch.

Rnd 9: Knit.

Rnd 10: *Ssk, k2, k2tog; rep from * to end of rnd—52 (56, 64) sts.

Rnd 11:

For smallest and largest sizes only: P2tog tbl, p1, p2tog, k3, *p3, k3; rep from * to last 8 sts, p2tog tbl, p1, p2tog, k3—48 (60) sts.

For middle size only: P2tog tbl, p1, p2tog, k3, *p3, k3; rep from * to end—54 sts.

Rnd 12: Work Rnd 4 of Crossed Stitch.

Rnd 13: Knit.

Rnd 14: *Ssk, k2, k2tog; rep from * to end—32 (36, 40) sts.

Rnd 15:

For smallest size only: K2, k2tog, p3, *k3, p3; rep from * to last 7 sts, k2, k2tog, p3—30 sts.

For middle size only: *K3, p3; rep from * to end.

For largest size only: Ssk, k1, k2tog, p3, *k3, p3; rep from * to last 8 sts, k3, p2tog tbl, p1, p2tog—36 sts.

Rnd 16: Work Rnd 8 of Crossed Stitch.

Rnd 17: Knit.

Rnd 18: *Ssk, k2, k2tog; rep from * to end—20 (24, 24) sts.

Rnd 19:

For smallest size only: P2tog tbl, p1, p2tog, k3, *p3, k3; rep from * to end—18 sts.

For middle and largest sizes only: *P3, k3; rep from * to end—24 sts.

Rnd 20: Work Rnd 4 of Crossed Stitch.

Rnd 21: Knit.

Rnd 22: *Ssk, k2, k2tog; rep from * to end—12 (16, 16) sts.

Rnd 23: *K2tog; rep from * to end—6 (8, 8) sts.

Cut yarn, leaving an 8"/20.5cm tail, weave through rem sts, cinch shut, secure on WS.

FINISHING

Weave in ends and block if desired.

Anu Baby Hat

DESIGNER: Carol J. Sulcoski   SKILL LEVEL: Easy

Fingering weight yarns have the ultimate versatility: If you're in a hurry (say, to whip out an adorable gift for a new baby), you can double-strand them for speed. This baby cap couldn't be simpler, but it also couldn't be cuter. It knits up in no time, using two strands of a gorgeous, hand-painted yarn.

FINISHED MEASUREMENTS

Circumference 13–16"/33–41cm, hat stretches to fit a range of sizes

MATERIALS AND TOOLS

Koigu Premium Painter's Palette (100% merino wool; 1.75oz/50g = 175yd/160m): 1 skein, color #P123B— approx 145yds/133m of fingering weight yarn 〔1〕

Knitting needles: 4.5mm (size 7 U.S.) 16" circular needle or size to obtain gauge

Spare 4.5mm (size 7 U.S.) circular needle or double pointed needles

Stitch marker

Tapestry needle

GAUGE

22 sts/30 rows = 4"/10cm in St st with 2 strands of yarn held tog

Always take time to check your gauge.

SPECIAL ABBREVIATION

S2kp: Slip 2 sts knitwise, k1, pass 2 slipped sts over knit st (2 sts decreased)

INSTRUCTIONS

With 2 strands of yarn held tog and circular needle, CO 96 sts. PM and join for working in the rnd, being careful not to twist.

Rnd 1: *K2, p2; rep from * to end.

Rep last rnd until ribbing measures 3"/8cm from beg.

Note: When circumference of hat gets too small to work comfortably on a single circular needle, beg using second circular needle or dpns.

Next rnd: *K2, k2tog, rep from * to end—72 sts.

Shape Crown:

Rnd 1: *K15, s2kp; rep from * to end—64 sts.

Rnd 2: Knit.

Rnd 3: *K13, s2kp; rep from * to end—56 sts.

Rnd 4: Knit.

Rnd 5: *K11, s2kp; rep from * to end—48 sts.

Rnd 6: Knit.

Rnd 7: *K9, s2kp; rep from * to end—40 sts.

Rnd 8: Knit.

Rnd 9: *K7, s2kp; rep from * to end—32 sts.

Rnd 10: Knit.

Rnd 11: *K5, s2kp; rep from * to end—24 sts.

Rnd 12: Knit.

Rnd 13: *K3, s2kp; rep from * to end—16 sts.

Rnd 14: Knit.

Rnd 15: *K2tog; rep from * to end—8 sts.

Cut yarn and draw through rem sts.

FINISHING

Weave in ends.

Two
SKEIN
PROJECTS

Thornapple Wrist Warmers

DESIGNER: Elizabeth Morrison   SKILL LEVEL: Experienced

These wrist warmers are a fun way to use yarn with long, gradual color changes for entrelac. The ribbed fabric and entrelac's bias structure allow them to fit a wide range of sizes. If you want the colors of the entrelac panel on each mitten to match, begin each panel at the same point in the yarn's repeat.

INSTRUCTIONS

Entrelac Panel (make 2):

With straight needles and A, loosely CO 46 sts. Stitch count includes 44 sts for 11 entrelac base triangles, each worked on 4 sts, plus 2 selvedge sts.

Next row: Purl.

11 Base Triangles:

K1 (selvedge st), then set up base triangles as follows:
First Triangle

Row 1 (RS): K1, turn.

Row 2 and all WS rows: Purl all sts in this section, turn.

Row 3: K2, turn.

Row 5: K3, turn.

Row 7: K4, do not turn. This completes first base triangle of 11 base triangles. Start next base triangle on next st. Rep Rows 1–7 for each of next 10 base triangles. End with k1 (selvedge st) after last base triangle.

FINISHED MEASUREMENTS

Length: 9½"/24cm

Wrist circumference (unstretched): Approx 5½"/14cm, to fit up to 7¼"/18cm wrist

MATERIALS AND TOOLS

Crystal Palace Sausalito (80% merino, 20% nylon; 1.75oz/50g = 198yd/181m): (A), 1 skein, color Fall Herbs #8107—approx 198yd/181m of fingering weight yarn (1)

Crystal Palace Mini Solid (80% merino, 20% nylon; 1.75oz/50g = 195yd/178m): (B), 1 skein, color Deep Loden #1104—approx 195yd/178m of fingering weight yarn (1)

Knitting needles: 2mm (size 0 U.S.) straight and double pointed needles or size to obtain gauge

Stitch markers

Tapestry needle

Stitch holder

GAUGE

Entrelac diamond = ½"/13mm square, using A.
12 sts/10 rows = 1"/3cm in 1x1 Rib (unstretched), using B

Always take time to check your gauge.

NOTES

1. The Sausalito yarn will appear quite different along different sections of the same ball. Sample wrist warmers were worked using similar-appearing sections for the entrelac panels.

2. One panel was rotated 180 degrees for finishing to make the panels appear to mirror one another on the two hands.

Tier 1—10 Full Diamonds and 2 Edge Triangles

LEFT EDGE TRIANGLE:

(Side triangles each include 1 selvedge st).

Row 1 (WS): P2, turn.

Row 2 (RS): Sl 1, M1, k1, turn.

Row 3: P2, p2tog, turn.

Row 4: Sl 1, k1, M1, k1, turn.

Row 5: P3, p2tog, turn.

Row 6: Sl 1, knit to last st, M1, k1 turn.

Row 7: P4, p2tog, do not turn. This completes the Left Edge Triangle.

TEN RIGHT SLANTING DIAMONDS:

Row 1(WS): With WS facing, pick up and purl 4 sts along the edge of the next triangle or diamond. Sl last st picked up onto the left needle and p2tog, turn.

Row 2: Sl 1, k4, turn.

Row 3: P3, p2tog, turn.

Rep Rows 2 and 3 until all sts from that base triangle or diamond have been worked together with newly-forming diamond section, ending after a purl row. Do not turn. Rep from Row 1, working a total of 10 complete diamonds in Tier 1. Do not turn after last diamond.

RIGHT EDGE TRIANGLE:

Row 1 (WS): With WS facing, pick up and purl 4 sts along the edge of the next triangle or diamond, knit selvedge st, turn.

Row 2: K1, k2tog, k2, turn.

Row 3: P4, turn.

Row 4: K1, k2tog, k1, turn.

Row 5: P3, turn.

Row 6: K1, k2tog, turn.

Row 7: P2, turn.

RS is now facing. K2, do not turn. The 2nd st will count as first st of next diamond section pick-up.

Tier 2—11 Left Slanting Diamonds:

Row 1 (RS): For first diamond only pick up and knit 3 more sts from edge of Tier 1 Right Edge Triangle. For subsequent diamonds, pick up and knit 4 sts, turn.

Row 2 (WS): Sl 1, p3, turn.

Row 3: K3, ssk, turn.

Rep Rows 2 and 3 until you have worked all the sts from the diamond in the lower tier with the new diamond forming in the current tier. Do not turn. Rep across forming 11 diamonds in Tier 2.

Rep Tier 1 once more.

FILLER TRIANGLES/BIND OFF:

Starting with 2 sts on RH needle from the Right Edge Triangle just completed, on WS, p2tog.

Row 1 (RS): Pick up and knit 4 sts along the edge of Right Edge Triangle just completed, turn.

Row 2: P3, p2tog, turn.

Row 3: Sl 1, k2, k2tog, turn.

Row 4: P2, p2tog, turn.

Row 5: Sl 1, k1, k2tog, turn.

Row 6: P1, p2tog, turn.

Row 7: Sl 1, k2tog, turn.

Row 8: P2tog, turn, ready to start next triangle on RS.

Rep Rows 1–8 across. On last Filler Triangle, after Row 8, BO last section st and final selvedge st.

Block entrelac panels well before starting main bodies of wrist warmers. Each panel should measure 1¾ x 9½"/4 x 24cm, blocked.

More About Entrelac

Although designer Elizabeth Morrison did a terrific job with pattern instructions for the center entrelac strips of the Thornapple Wristers, entrelac is a complex technique. If you'd like some background information on entrelac, or are intrigued and want to do more, two recent (and excellent) books on the technique are: *Entrelac* by Rosemary Drysdale (Sixth & Spring, 2010) and *Entrée to Entrelac* by Gwen Bortner (XRX Books, 2010).

Right Hand Main Body:

With straight needles and B, loosely CO 45 sts.

Work in 1x1 Rib for 6"/15cm, ending with a WS row.

THUMB GUSSET:

Set up row (RS): Work first 9 sts in established rib, PM, M1, p1, k1, p1, M1, PM, work inestablished rib to end.

Row 1 (WS): Work in established rib, incorporating all newly-formed sts into ribbing on thumb gusset, between markers.

Row 2 (RS): Work in established rib to first marker, sl marker, M1, work established rib to next marker, M1, sl marker, work to end.

Rep Rows 1 and 2 until there are 23 sts between markers, ending with a WS row—65 sts.

Next row (RS): Work to first marker, remove marker, place next 23 sts onto a holder for thumb, remove other marker, CO 3 sts over gap, work in established rib to end.

Work in established rib until piece measures 9½"/24cm and is same length as entrelac panels.

BO loosely.

THUMB:

With dpns, place 23 sts from holder on 2 needles. Using a 3rd needle, join yarn, and pick up and knit 3 sts from cast-on over thumb gusset gap. Distribute sts evenly on needles. Work in 1x1 Rib for 7 rnds.

BO loosely.

Left Hand Main Body:

Work as for Right Hand Main Body to thumb gusset.

THUMB GUSSET:

Set up row (RS): Work first 33 sts in established rib, PM, M1, p1, k1, p1, M1, PM, work in established rib to end.

Resume following Right Hand instructions to end.

FINISHING

Seam one blocked entrelac panel to one main body section. Rep for other wrist warmer. Weave in ends.

Fair Isle Peacock Hat

DESIGNER: Tanis Gray   SKILL LEVEL: Intermediate

An ideal project for one variegated and one solid color yarn, this "faux isle" hat looks like more work than it really is. An illusion that many different colored yarns were used when it's the variegated doing the work for you will wow knitters and non-knitters alike.

INSTRUCTIONS

Brim:

With circular needle and A, CO 150 sts. PM and join for working in the rnd, being careful not to twist.

Work in Corrugated Rib until piece measures 2"/5cm from CO edge.

Beg Chart:

Knit Rows 1–39 of chart.

Note: You will rep the 50 sts of each row of the chart a total of 3 times in each rnd.

FINISHED MEASUREMENTS

Circumference: 22"/56cm

MATERIALS AND TOOLS

Louet Gems Fingering (100% merino wool; 1.75oz/50g = 185yd/169m): (A), 1 skein, color black #22—approx 148yd/135m of fingering weight yarn (1)

Skacel Zauberball (75% superwash wool, 25% nylon; 3.5oz/100g = 459yd/420m): (B),1 skein, color #1963—approx 73yds/67m of fingering weight yarn (1)

Knitting needles: 2.75mm (size 2 U.S.) double pointed needles or size to obtain gauge

2.75mm (size 2 U.S.) 16" circular needle

Stitch marker

Tapestry needle

GAUGE

31 sts/36 rows = 4½"/11cm in pattern using (A and B)

Always take time to check your gauge.

PATTERN STITCHES

Corrugated Rib:

Rnd 1: *With A, k1, with B, p1; rep from * to end.

Rep Rnd 1 for pat.

Shape Crown:

Rnd 1 (dec): *K2tog; rep from * to end—75 sts.

Rnd 2: Knit.

Rnd 3 (dec): *K2tog; rep from * to last st, k1—38 sts.

Rnd 4: Knit.

Rnd 5 (dec): Rep Rnd 1—19 sts.

Cut yarn, leaving an 8"/20.5cm tail, weave through
rem sts, cinch shut, secure on WS.

FINISHING
Weave in ends. Block.

Chart

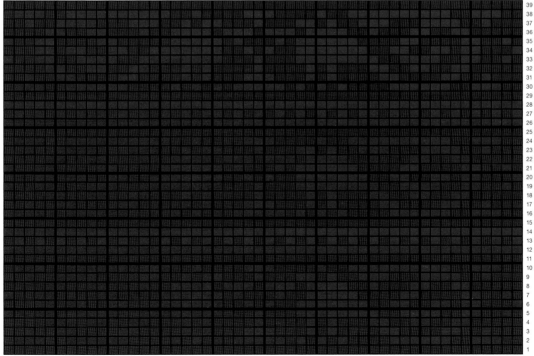

Roxy Legwarmers

DESIGNER: Barb Brown **SKILL LEVEL:** Intermediate

Inspired by the roller derby, these legwarmers feature stranded colorwork with calf shaping cleverly worked into the pattern. The legwarmers are great for layering, as they can be worn over stockings, bare legs, or socks. The calf shaping panel can be worn in the front for a naughty look, on the side for a more classic feel, or in the back for a sporty touch—and the I-cord is a rakish way to prevent sagging.

INSTRUCTIONS

Top Ribbing:

With smaller needles and A, CO 90 (96, 102) sts. PM for beg of rnd, and join for working in the rnd, being careful not to twist.

Ribbing Rnd: *K2, p1; rep from * to end.

Rep last rnd 14 more times.

Change to larger needles.

Next Rnd: With A, knit.

I-Cord Casing:

Rnd 1: With B, *k2, sl 1; rep from * to end.

Rnd 2: With B, *p2, sl 1wyib; rep from * to end.

Rnds 3 and 4: Rep Rnds 1 and 2.

Rnd 5: Rep Rnd 1.

Cut B.

FINISHED MEASUREMENTS

Circumference: 10 (10½, 11)"/25 (26, 28)cm

Height: 17"/43cm

Note: Legwarmers will fit legs up to 2"/5cm larger than actual circumference of leg.

MATERIALS AND TOOLS

Black Bunny Fibers Plump (80% superwash merino, 20% nylon; 3.5oz/100g = 400yd/366m); (A), 1 skein, color Smashing—400yd/366m of fingering weight yarn **1**

Black Bunny Fibers CashMerino Sock (80% superwash merino, 10% cashmere, 10% nylon; 3.5oz/100g = 425yd/389m); (B), 1 skein, color Midnight—400yd/366m of fingering weight yarn **1**

Knitting needles: 3.25mm (size 3 U.S.) double pointed needles, or size to obtain gauge

2.75mm (size 2 U.S.) double pointed needles, or one size smaller than above

Stitch markers

Tapestry needle

GAUGE

36 sts/36 rows = 4"/10cm in chart pattern

Always take time to check your gauge.

Next Rnd: With A, knit.

Change to smaller needles, work Ribbing Rnd (2x1 Rib) for 10 rnds.

Change to larger needles.

Next rnd: Knit, inc 2 sts evenly around—92 (98, 104) sts.

Beg Charts:

Work Chart A (Shaping) over first 31 sts, work rep of Chart B to last st of rnd, work Chart C.

When shaping is complete, cont pattern as established, working the 5 rem sts from Chart 1 until work measures 17"/43cm from beg or 2"/5cm less than desired total length—66 (72, 78) sts rem.

Change to smaller needles and A. Work Ribbing Rnd (2x1 Rib) for 15 rnds.

Bind-off for Cuff:

With knitted cast on, *CO 2 sts to the left needle, BO 4 sts (the 2 sts just cast on, plus the next 2 sts), sl rem 1 st from the RH needle back to the LH needle; rep from * until all sts have been bound off.

Make second legwarmer to match.

FINISHING

I-Cord Tie for top: With smaller needles, CO 2 sts and work in I-cord for 22 (23, 24)"/56 (58, 61)cm. Cut yarn and fasten off sts.

Weave in ends and thread I-Cord through I-Cord casing, beg at center back slipped st. Block as desired.

Chart A

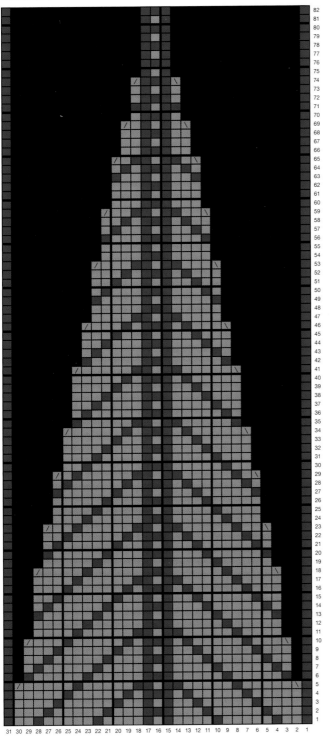

Chart B

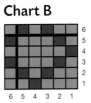

Chart C

Stitch Key

☐ knit

\ ssk

/ k2tog

■ no stitch

Kitteh Mittens

DESIGNER: Wendy D. Johnson   **SKILL LEVEL:** Intermediate

Fans of stranded knitting and cats alike will adore this charming project. Since mittens take almost as much abuse as socks, the durable, machine-wash friendly qualities of sock yarn come in handy.

FINISHED MEASUREMENTS

Circumference: 8"/20cm

Length (from cuff to tip): 10½"/27cm

MATERIALS AND TOOLS

The Loopy Ewe Solid Series (100% superwash merino wool; 2oz/55g = 220yd/201m): (A), 1 skein, color Cerulean #48-69; (B), 1 skein, color Coffee #14-34—approx 250yd/229m of fingering weight yarn

Knitting needles: Two sets of 2.75mm (size 2 U.S.) 24" circular and one set of double pointed needles, or size to obtain gauge

Stitch markers

Tapestry needle

Stitch holders

GAUGE

36 sts/36 rows = 4"/10cm in two-color St st

Always take time to check your gauge.

INSTRUCTIONS

Left Hand:

With A, cast on 54 sts over 2 circular needles (22 on one needle for the palm and 32 on the 2nd needle for the back of hand) and join for working in the rnd, being careful not to twist.

Ribbing rnd: *With A, k1, with B, p1; rep from * to end.

Rep this rnd for 1x1 Corrugated Rib, using A for knit sts and B for purl sts. Work a total of 20 rnds of ribbing.

BEGIN LEFT HAND CHART:

Rnd 1: Work the first row of the chart, knitting all sts, increasing 4 sts over the palm and 4 sts over the back of hand—62 sts.

Work the 26 sts for the palm on one needle and the 36 sts for the back of hand on the other. Work increases for the thumb gusset as indicated on the chart by inserting the tip of your needle into the bar

between 2 sts and knitting it up into a new st. When you reach the round above the heavy line on the chart across the 13 thumb gusset sts, slip these 13 sts to a holder, cast on 13 sts over the gap, and continue knitting in pat.

When you reach the first set of decreases at the top of the mitten, work as follows:

Work 1 chart st, ssk, work across to the next dec in the pat, k2tog, work 3 chart sts, ssk, work across to the next dec in the pat, k2tog, work 2 chart sts.

Continue in this manner until you complete the chart and 14 sts remain on each needle. Graft these sts together or do a three-needle bind-off to close the top of the mitten.

WORK THE THUMB:

Place the 13 thumb sts from the holder on a dpn. Work across the first 15 sts of the first row of the thumb chart as follows: pick up and work 1 st in the gap before the sts on the dpn, then work across the 13 sts on the needle, pick up and work 1 st in the gap

after the 13 sts on the dpn. Using another dpn, pick up and knit 15 sts along the cast-on edge, working them according to the last 15 sts of the first row of the thumb chart. You have a total of 30 thumb sts. Arrange these sts over 3 dpns and work all rnds of the thumb chart. When you reach the first set of decreases at the top of the thumb, work as follows:

Ssk, work across to the next dec, k2tog, ssk, work across to the next dec, k2tog.

Continue in this manner until chart is complete—6 sts rem. Cut the working yarns and thread the B yarn through these 6 sts tightly. Weave in ends.

Right Hand:

Work the same as the Left Hand, using the Right Hand Chart. After completing the hand, work the thumb as described above.

FINISHING

Weave in ends. Block.

Thumb Chart

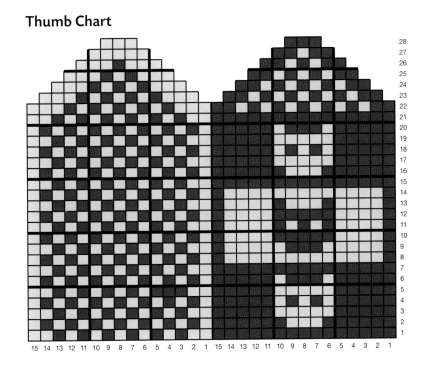

28
27
26
25
24
23
22
21
20
19
18
17
16
15
14
13
12
11
10
9
8
7
6
5
4
3
2
1

15 14 13 12 11 10 9 8 7 6 5 4 3 2 1   15 14 13 12 11 10 9 8 7 6 5 4 3 2 1

Left Hand Chart

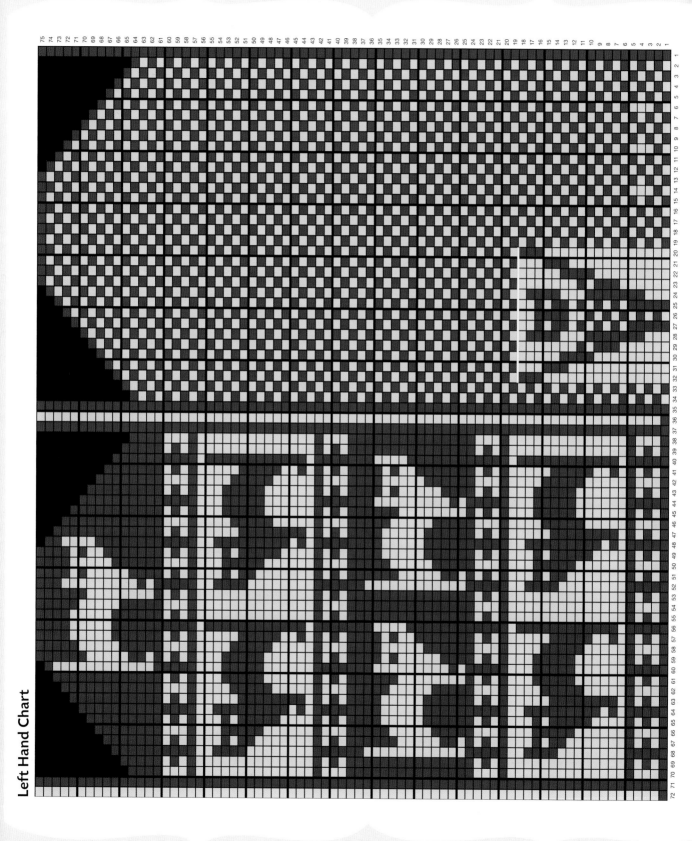

Right Hand Chart

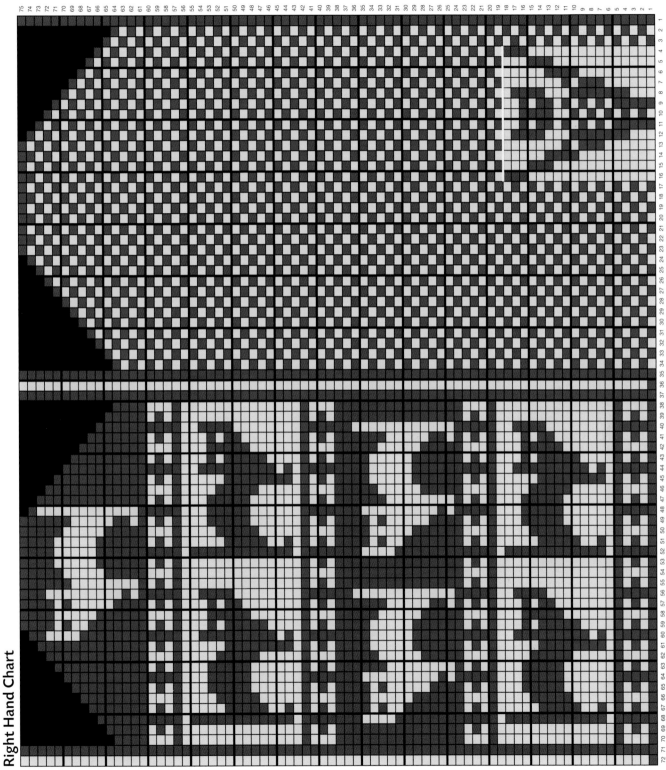

Cushington Square Pillow

DESIGNER: Barb Brown   SKILL LEVEL: Intermediate

Inspired by an old woven tapestry, this cushion adds a touch of sophistication to any room. The reverse side of offset stripes (page 91) gives a different look, and the button top makes it easy to remove the cover for cleaning.

INSTRUCTIONS

With B, CO 218 sts.

PM and join for working in the rnd, being careful not to twist.

Knit 4 rnds.

Next rnd: K2 with B, work Chart A over the next 105 sts (work sts 1 to 42 twice, then 1 to 21 once), k4 with B, work Chart B over next 105 sts, k2 with B.

Note: 34 rows are 1 rep of the pat on Chart A, and 10 rows are 1 rep of Chart B.

Work 3 full reps of Chart A.

Back Buttonband:

With A only, and working back and forth, knit 10 rows (Garter st) on back 109 sts.

With A, BO these 109 sts. Cut A.

FINISHED MEASUREMENTS

To fit 14"/36cm square pillow form

MATERIALS AND TOOLS

Black Bunny Fibers Falkland Softsilk Sock (50% Falkland wool, 50% silk; 3.5oz/100g = 425yd/389m): (A), 1 skein, color Cream; (B), 1 skein, color Chestnut—approx 500yd/457m of fingering weight yarn ❶

Knitting needles: 3.25mm (size 3 U.S.) or size to obtain gauge

Stitch marker

Tapestry needle

6 buttons, ¼"/6mm diameter

GAUGE

32 sts/32 rows = 4"/10cm in Chart A

Always take time to check your gauge.

Flawless Fair Isle

Many knitters are needlessly intimidated by stranded knitting (often referred to as "Fair Isle knitting," whether or not the motifs originated from the Shetland Isles). Barb Brown's Cushington Square pillow cover is a good project if you're new to stranded knitting since no shaping or steeking is required. If you haven't done much stranded knitting, start by figuring out a comfortable way to hold the two strands of yarn while you're working with them. Some knitters hold one strand in each hand, while others hold both strands in the same hand. The precise method you use isn't as important as finding one that works for you and being consistent with it. Pay attention to how tightly or loosely you are stranding the yarn across the wrong side of the work. If you pull the yarn too tight, the knitting will bunch together and distort the pattern; too loose and you'll get holes in the fabric where the colors meet. Most beginners tend to pull their yarn tighter than it needs to be, so if you find you're doing so, stop every couple of stitches and spread out your stitches across the needle to counteract this tendency. As with most things, practice will pay off—and a good blocking never hurt, either!

Front Flap:

Set Up: With WS of front facing and A, purl, inc 1 st—110 sts.

Row 1a (RS): With A, *sl 1, k1; rep from * to end.

Row 1b (RS): Slide work back to beg of needle; with B, knit.

Row 2a (WS): With A, *sl 1, p1; rep from * to end.

Row 2b (WS): Slide work back to beg of needle; with B, purl.

Rep Rows 1a–2b until flap measures 2"/5cm, ending with a WS row.

Next 2 rows: With A, knit.

Next (buttonhole) row (RS): K6, [BO 3, k16] 5 times, BO 3, k4, k2tog—91 sts.

BO loosely, when the bind off for each buttonhole is reached, insert left needle into st on right needle. Wrap yarn around right needle as if to knit, draw through, repeat total of 3 times (like chain stitch in crochet).

FINISHING

Weave in ends. Sew lower seam. Sew buttons to back button band opposite buttonholes on front flap. Wash and block to size.

Chart A (Front)

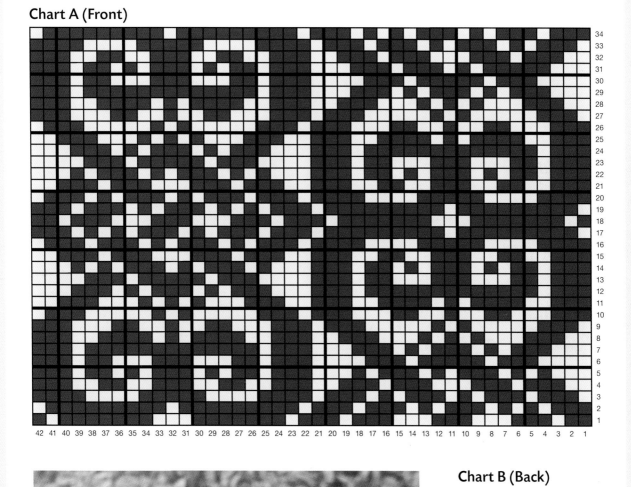

Chart B (Back)

Stitch Key

☐ knit

■ knit

Furbelow Shawl

DESIGNER: Carol J. Sulcoski   **SKILL LEVEL:** Easy

Sometimes a sock yarn is just so pretty you can't stand to put it on your feet. This cashmere-blend hand-paint, in a soft sage green color, is one such skein; its buttery-soft hand and relatively high cashmere content beg to be worn next to the face, where you can cuddle them. Ruffles in a coordinating silk-mohair blend add a touch of whimsy.

PATTERN STITCH

Textured Stripe:

Row 1 (RS): K3, yo, knit to marker, yo, sl marker, k2, sl marker, yo, knit to last 3 sts, yo, k3.
Row 2: K3, purl to marker, sl marker, k2, sl marker, purl to last 3 sts, k3.

Rows 3–8: Rep Rows 1 and 2 three times.

Row 9: K3, yo, purl to marker, yo, sl marker, k2, sl marker, yo, purl to last 3 sts, yo, k3.

Row 10: K3, knit to marker, sl marker, k2, sl marker, knit to last 3 sts, k3.

Rows 11–16: Rep Rows 9 and 10 three times.

Rep Rows 1-16 for pat.

FINISHED MEASUREMENTS

Width (across top edge): 42"/107cm, not including ruffle

Length (at center back): 20"/51cm

MATERIALS AND TOOLS

Artyarns Cashmere Sock (67% cashmere, 25% wool, 8% nylon; 1.75oz/50g = 160yd/ 146m): (A) 3 skeins, color #2292—approx 425yd/389m of sport weight yarn (2)

Artyarns Silk Mohair (60% mohair, 40% silk; 0.9oz/25g = 312yd/285m): (B) 1 skein, color #105—approx 250 yds/228m of lace weight yarn (0)

Knitting needles: 4.0mm (size 6 U.S.) 32" circular needle or size to obtain gauge

Stitch markers

Tapestry needle

GAUGE

20 sts/26 rows = 4"/10cm in Textured Stripe with A, after blocking

Always take time to check your gauge.

SPECIAL ABBREVIATION

Kfb: Knit in the front & back of the stitch—1 st increased.

INSTRUCTIONS

With A, CO 4 sts, PM, CO 2 sts, PM, CO 4 sts—10 sts.

Knit 1 row.

Next row (RS): K2, yo, k2, yo, sl marker, k2, sl marker, yo, k2, yo, k2—14 sts.

Knit 1 row.

Next row (RS): K3, yo, knit to marker, yo, sl marker, k2, sl marker, yo, knit to last 3 sts, yo, k3—18 sts.

Knit 1 row.

Rep the last 2 rows one more time—22 sts.

Work 7 repeats of Textured Stripe—246 sts.

Knit 8 rows.

Ruffle Edging:

Row 1 (RS): With B, *k1, kfb; rep from * to end of row—492 sts.

Row 2 (WS): Purl.

Rep these 2 rows 2 more times.

Work 6 rows in St st.

BO off all sts knitwise.

FINISHING

Weave in ends and block main section of shawl, being careful not to crush ruffle.

Gumdrop Raglan

DESIGNER: Carol J. Sulcoski   **SKILL LEVEL:** Easy

Self-patterning yarn is just right for the sleeves of this adorable raglan sweater. The soft hand and machine washability of sock yarn make it an especially good choice for young children's garments. Whether you opt for machine-dyed yarn or a striping hand-paint, this sweater is full of charm.

SPECIAL ABBREVIATIONS

M1L (make 1 left-slanting): Pick up horizontal bar between sts by inserting right-hand needle from front to back and slipping it onto left needle; knit this st through the back loop.

M1R (make 1 right-slanting): Pick up horizontal bar between sts by inserting right-hand needle from back to front, and slipping it onto left needle; knit this st through the front loop.

MC (mock cable): K2tog but do not slip off left-hand needle, k1 through the center of the same 2 sts, slip both sts off needle.

PATTERN STITCHES

Mock Cable Ribbing I – worked back and forth in rows (multiple of 4 sts + 2):

Rows 1, 2 and 4: K1, *k2, p2; rep from * to last st, k1.

FINISHED MEASUREMENTS

Chest: 20 (22, 24, 27, 30)"/51 (56, 61, 69, 76)cm

Length (from lower edge to shoulder): 11½ (12¾, 14¼, 15¾, 17¾)"/29 (32, 36, 40, 45)cm

MATERIALS AND TOOLS

Version 1 (pink; shown in smallest size): Lion Brand Sock-Ease (75% wool, 25% nylon; 3.5oz/100g = 438yd/400m): (A), 1 (2, 2, 2, 3) skeins, color Lollipop #139; (B), 1 (1, 2, 2, 3) skeins, color Cotton Candy #205

Version 2 (violet/green; shown in largest size): Lorna's Laces Shepherd Sock (80% superwash merrno/20% nylon; 3.5oz/100g = 430yd/393m): (A), 1 (1, 1, 2, 2) skeins, color Violet; (B), 1 (1, 1, 2, 2) skeins, color Jungle Stripe

Approximate yardage for either version: 475 (625, 775, 975, 1150)yd/434 (572, 709, 892, 1052)m of fingering weight yarn

Knitting needles: 3.25mm (size 3 U.S.) needles or size to obtain gauge

2.75mm (size 2 U.S.) straight and 16" circular needles or one size smaller than above

Stitch marker

Stitch holder

Tapestry needle

GAUGE

28 sts/36 rows = 4"/10cm in St st

Always take time to check your gauge.

Row 3: K1, *MC, p2; rep from * to last st, k1.

Rep Rows 1-4 for pat.

Mock Cable Ribbing II – worked in rnds (multiple of 4 sts):

Rnds 1, 2 and 4: *K2, p2; rep from * to end.

Rnd 3: *MC, p2, rep from * to end.

Rep Rows 1-4 for pat.

INSTRUCTIONS

Back:

With smaller straight needles and A, CO 70 (78, 86, 94, 106) sts.

Set-up row (WS): K1, *k2, p2; rep from * to last st, k1.

Work 3 reps of Mock Cable Ribbing I.

Change to larger needles and St st.

Work in St st until back measures 7½ (8¼, 9, 9¾, 11)"/19 (21, 23, 25, 28)cm from beg.

RAGLAN ARMHOLE SHAPING:

BO 5 sts at beg of next 2 rows—60 (68, 76, 84, 96) sts.

For first three sizes only:

Next (dec) row (RS): K4, ssk, knit to last 6 sts, k2tog, k4—58 (66, 74) sts.

Next (dec) row (WS): P4, p2tog, purl to last 6 sts, p2tog tbl, p4—56 (64, 72) sts.

Work these 2 rows 3 (2, 1) more times—44 (56, 68) sts.

FOR ALL SIZES:

Next (dec) row (RS): K4, ssk, knit to last 6 sts, k2tog, k4—42 (54, 66, 82, 94) sts.

Next row: Purl.

Rep these 2 rows 11 (15, 19, 26, 30) more times—20 (24, 28, 30, 34) sts rem.

SHOULDER AND NECK:

BO 6 (6, 7, 7, 8) sts, knit next 8 (12, 14, 16, 18) sts and place on holder for neck, BO 6 (6, 7, 7, 8) sts.

Front:

Work as for back, and at the same time, when armhole measures 1¾ (2¼, 3, 4, 4¾)/4 (6, 8, 10, 12) cm from bound-off armhole sts, begin neck shaping while cont to work all raglan decreases as for Back.

Next row (RS): Knit to center 8 (8, 10, 12, 14) sts, BO center 8 (8, 10, 12, 14) sts, then joining a second ball of yarn, knit to end of row.

Working both sides at same time with separate balls of yarn, dec 1 st at each side of neck 3 times. When all raglan and neckline decs are complete, cont without further dec until front shoulders are same size as back shoulders.

BO rem 3 (5, 6, 6, 7) sts.

Sleeves (make 2):

With smaller straight needles and A, cast on 42 (46, 46, 50, 50) sts.

Set-up row (WS): K1, *k2, p2; rep from * to last st, k1.

Work 3 reps of Mock Cable Ribbing I.

Change to larger needles and B, and knit 1 row, then purl 1 row.

Next (inc) row: K2, M1R, knit to last 4 sts, M1L, k2—44 (48, 48, 52, 52) sts.

Work 1 (1, 1, 3, 5) rows in St st.

Rep these 2 (2, 2, 4, 6) rows 11 (11, 12, 11, 13) more times—66 (70, 72, 74, 78) sts.

If necessary, work without further increases until sleeve measures 4½ (6¾, 9, 11¼, 13½)"/11 (17, 23, 29, 34)cm from cast-on edge.

RAGLAN SHAPING:

BO 5 sts at beg of next 2 rows—56 (60, 62, 64, 68) sts.

FOR FIRST THREE SIZES ONLY:

Next (dec) row (RS): K4, ssk, knit to last 6 sts, k2tog, k4—54 (58, 60) sts.

Next (dec) row (WS): P4, p2tog, purl to last 6 sts, p2tog tbl, p4—52 (56, 58) sts.

Work these 2 rows 3 (2, 1) more times—40 (48, 54) sts.

FOR ALL SIZES:

Next (dec) row (RS): K4, ssk, knit to last 6 sts, k2tog, k4—38 (46, 52, 62, 66) sts.

Next row: Purl.

Rep these 2 rows 11 (15, 19, 26, 30) more times—16 (16, 14, 10, 6) sts.

If necessary, work without further increases until sleeve measures 4 (4½, 5¼, 6, 6¾)"/10 (11, 13, 15, 17) cm from bound-off sts at underarm.

BO all rem sts.

FINISHING

Block pieces.

Sew sleeves to front and back, matching raglan edges, then sew side and underarm seams.

Transfer 8 (12, 14, 16, 18) back neck sts onto circular needle, and with A, knit. Cont working around neck, picking up 12 (15, 18, 21, 24) sts across left side of neckline, picking up 8 (10, 12, 14, 18) sts across bound-off neck sts, and picking up 12 (15, 18, 21, 24) sts across right side of neckline—40 (52, 62, 72, 84) sts.

Note: Exact number of sts picked up is not as important as ensuring that sweater does not ripple or gap where stitches are picked up. If sweater ripples, pick up fewer sts; if it gaps, pick up more. Total number of sts must be a multiple of 4.

PM and join for working in the rnd. Work 3 reps of Mock Cable Ribbing II, then bind off all sts in pat. Weave in ends.

Back:

Place 94 (106, 116, 128) sts back on needle.

Beg with a WS row, [p1, k1] 2 times, p1, PM, p37 (43, 48, 54), PM, [p1, k1] 2 times, p2, [k1, p1] 2 times, PM, p37 (43, 48, 54), PM, [p1, k1] 2 times, p1.

Next (dec) row: K5, sl marker, ssk, knit to 2 sts before last marker, k2tog, sl marker, knit to end—92 (104, 114, 126) sts.

Next row: [P1, k1] 2 times, p1, sl marker, purl to next marker, sl marker, [p1, k1] 2 times, p2, [k1, p1] 2 times, sl marker, purl to last marker, sl marker, [p1, k1] 2 times, p1.

Rep the last 2 rows 1 time—90 (102, 112, 124) sts.

Next row (work dec and divide work): K5, sl marker, ssk, knit to second marker, sl marker, k5, place rem 45 (51, 56, 62) sts on holder for Left Back, turn, cont on rem 44 (50, 55, 61) sts for Right Back.

RIGHT BACK:

Next row: Cont in Broken Rib to marker, sl marker, purl to next marker, sl marker, cont in Broken Rib to end.

Cont to work the 5 sts outside markers in Broken Rib.

Next (dec) row (RS): K5, sl marker, ssk, knit to end—43 (49, 54, 60) sts.

Rep this dec row every RS row 9 (17, 21, 28) times, then every 4th row 10 (7, 7, 5) times—24 (25, 26, 27) sts.

Next WS row: BO 19 (20, 21, 22) sts, place rem 5 sts on holder.

LEFT BACK:

Place 45 (51, 56, 62) sts back on needle.

Beg with a RS row.

Next (dec) row (RS): Knit to 2 sts before 2nd marker, k2tog, knit to end—44 (50, 55, 61) sts.

Rep this dec row every RS row 10 (18, 22, 29) times more, then every 4th row 10 (7, 7, 5) times, keeping 5 sts outside markers in Broken Rib—24 (25, 26, 27) sts.

Next RS row, BO 19 (20, 21, 22) sts, place rem 5 sts on holder.

FINISHING

Connect 5 edge sts of fronts to 5 edge sts of backs with 3 needle bind off.

Collar:

With RS facing, pick up and knit 18 (19, 20 21) sts along left back neck, 60 (64, 66, 68) sts along front neck, 18 (19, 20, 21) sts along right back neck, then cast on 8 sts—104 (110, 114, 118) sts.

Knit back and forth, do not join.

Work 4 rows in Broken Rib.

Next (buttonhole) row (RS): Work to last 6 sts, k2tog, yo, knit to end.

Rep this buttonhole row every 1"/3cm 2 times more.

Cont in Broken Rib until collar is 3"/8cm. BO.

Weave in ends, block. Sew 3 buttons to left side of collar to correspond to buttonholes on right.

Lizalu Blanket

DESIGNER: Carol J. Sulcoski   SKILL LEVEL: Easy

Whether you deliberately select coordinating colorways for this patchwork-style blanket, or use up oddballs left over from other projects, you'll end up with a cozy, warm and undeniably fun project. Each column of eight blocks is knit as a continuous strip, with Garter stitch rows of a main color acting as dividers. You then join the strips and add a Garter stitch edging. The individual strips are very portable and make good travel projects.

INSTRUCTIONS

Individual strip (make 12):

With first square color, CO 35 sts.

Work in St st until piece measures 5"/13cm long.

*Change to A and knit 4 rows.

Change to next square color, and work in St st for 5"/13cm.

Rep from * until you have worked a total of 8 different colored blocks.

BO all sts.

Weave in ends and block as desired.

FINISHED MEASUREMENTS

Individual blocks: Approx 5"/13cm square

Individual strips: Approx 42"/107cm long x 5"/13cm wide

Finished blanket: Approx 44"/112cm long x 62"/157cm wide

MATERIALS AND TOOLS

Regia 4-ply (75% superwash wool/25% nylon; 1.75oz/50g = 230yd/210m): (A), 5 skeins, color Anthracite Marl #522—approx 1000yd/914m of fingering weight yarn

Assorted remnants of sock yarn; each individual block takes approx 12-15g/75–100yd/69–91m of fingering weight yarn

Knitting needles: 3.25mm (size 4 U.S.) 36" circular needles or size to obtain gauge

Stitch marker

Size 3.25mm (size D-3 U.S.) crochet hook

Tapestry needle

GAUGE

28 sts/40 rows = 4"/10cm in St st

Always take time to check your gauge.

Note: Blanket consists of 12 strips, each of which is knit individually. Strips are sewn together and stitches picked up along the edge for Garter st edging.

Joining Strips

There are lots of ways to join squares or strips into a blanket. The strips that make up the Lizalu blanket were joined together using a crochet slip-stitch. Begin with a crochet hook that is comparable in size to the knitting needles you used to make the strips. Place the strips you are joining with the right sides together, facing in, and the wrong sides facing outward. Slip the hook into just one loop from the first stitch on each strip (if you put your hook through 2 loops on both strips the seam will be very bulky and noticeable). Pull the yarn through the loops. You will have a loop remaining on the needle. Now slip the hook into one loop from each of the next stitches on each strip, and pull the yarn through both loops and the stitch remaining on your needle. Continue in this way all the way across. When you reach the end of the strips, break off the yarn and slip it through the last stitch.

FINISHING

When 12 strips are completed, lay out individual strips side by side, re-arranging if necessary until you are satisfied with layout.

With crochet hook and A, slip stitch strips together in the chosen order along long vertical edges. Weave in additional ends.

EDGING

With circular needle and A, pick up approx 280 sts across one of the shorter edges of blanket.

Knit 10 rows.

BO all sts loosely.

Rep on other short edge.

With circular needle and A, pick up approx 440 sts across one of the longer edges of blanket.

Knit 10 rows. Repeat on other long edge.

BO all sts loosely.

Weave in ends and steam block.

All sorts of sock yarns were used to make squares in the Lizalu Blanket: machine-dyed solids, hand-painted solids, multicolor hand-paints, space-dyed yarns, slow self-stripers and self-patterning yarns. If you look closely, you might recognize some of the yarns in other projects in this book!

Nuit Blanche Stole and Scarf

DESIGNER: Véronik Avery   SKILL LEVEL: Intermediate

Slip-stitch patterns do a brilliant job of creating colorful patterns, and sock yarns are a perfect choice, as the resulting fabric is lightweight and retains drape. A lovely hand-painted yarn is used in the scarf version, where the slipped stitches help move the colors around and avoid pooling or splotchy effects. Of course, the design is just as lovely using solid yarns, as in the larger stole pattern.

INSTRUCTIONS FOR STOLE

Using a provisional method and A1, CO 57 sts.

Purl 1 WS row.

Set up pattern:

Row 1 (RS): Sl 1 wyib (selvedge st), work Row 1 of Slip Stitch Chart to last st, end k1 (selvedge st).

Row 2 (WS): Sl 1 wyif (selvedge st), work Row 2 of Slip Stitch Chart to last st, end p1 (selvedge st).

FINISHED MEASUREMENTS

Stole: Approx 14½"/37cm x 62"/157cm, after blocking

Scarf: Approx 7" (18cm) by 52"/132cm, after blocking

MATERIALS AND TOOLS

Stole: St-Denis Boreale (100% wool; 1.75oz/50g = 225yd/206m): 1 ball each of (A1) color Espresso #1238, (B1) color Aurora #1205, (A2) color Elephant #1275, (B2) color Champagne #1216, (A3) color Pewter #1209 and (B3) color Honey Glaze #1212—approx 150yd/137m each of six fingering weight yarns ❶

Scarf: Tanis Fiber Arts Purple Label Cashmere Sock (70% superwash merino wool, 20% cashmere, 10% nylon; 4oz/115g = 400yd/365m): 1 skein each of (A) color Stormy and color Soot (B)—approx 250yd/229m each of two fingering weight yarns ❶

Knitting needles: 4mm (size 6 U.S.) needles or size to obtain gauge

Waste yarn and crochet hook (if desired, for provisional cast-on)

Tapestry needle

Stitch markers

6 buttons, ⅝"/16mm diameter

GAUGE

23 sts/38 rows = 4"/10cm in Slip Stitch, before blocking

23 sts/31 rows = 4"/10cm in Slip Stitch, after blocking

Always take time to check your gauge.

Maintaining selvedge sts throughout, cont in established pat, changing colors as follows:

Rows 1–24: A1 and B1.

Rows 25–48: A2 and B2.

Rows 49–60: A1 and B1.

Rows 61–84: A3 and B3.

Rows 85–96: A1 and B1.

Rows 97–120: A2 and B2.

Rows 121–324: A1 and B1.

Rows 325–348: A2 and B2.

Rows 349–360: A1 and B1.

Rows 361–384: A3 and B3.

Rows 385–396: A1 and B1.

Rows 397–420: A2 and B2.

Rows 421–444: A1 and B1.

Maintaining selvedge sts, knit 1 row.

Leave sts on needle but do not cut yarn.

FINISHING

PM for beg of rnd. With RS facing and A1, pick up and knit 1 st through every slipped stitch along left side of stole (222 sts), PM; carefully undo provisional cast-on edge, place resulting sts on left needle and knit across (56 sts), PM; pick up and knit along right edge as for left side of stole (222 sts), PM, k57—557 sts.

Note: All M1 increases on rnd 1 should be worked as backward loops.

Rnd 1: (left edge) K2, *p1, M1, p1, k1, M1, k1; rep from * to last 4 sts before next marker, p1, M1, p1, k2; (bottom edge) sl marker, k2, p1, M1, p1, *k3, p3; rep from * to 4 sts before next marker, k4; (right edge) sl marker, k2, *p1, M1, p1, k1, M1, k1; rep from * to last 4 sts before next marker, p1, M1, p1, k2; (top edge) sl marker, k2, *p3, k3; rep from * to last st, k1.

Rnd 2: *K2, yo, work in established 3x3 Rib to 2 sts before next marker, yo, k2; rep from * 3 times more.

Rnd 3: Work even, incorporating the yarnovers into 3x3 Rib.

Rep Rnds 2 and 3 nine more times, changing colors as follows:

Rnds 4 and 5: A1.

Rnds 6 and 7: B3.

Rnds 8 and 9: A1.

Rnds 10–13: B1.

Rnds 14–21: A1.

BO all sts purlwise.

Block to finished measurements. Weave in ends.

INSTRUCTIONS FOR SCARF

Using a provisional method and A, CO 33 sts.

Purl 1 WS row.

Set up pattern:

Row 1: Sl 1 wyib (selvedge st), work Row 1 of Slip Stitch Chart to last st, end k1 (selvedge st).

Row 2: Sl 1 wyif (selvedge st), work Row 2 of Slip Stitch Chart to last st, end p1 (selvedge st).

Maintaining selvedge sts throughout, cont in established pat until scarf is approx 43"/109cm long ending having just worked 2 rows with B. Maintaining selvedge sts, knit 1 row with B. Leave sts on needle but do not cut yarn.

FINISHING

PM for beg of rnd. With RS facing and A, pick up and knit 1 st through every slipped stitch along left side of scarf (approx 204 sts), PM; carefully undo provisional cast-on edge, place resulting sts on left needle and knit across (32 sts), PM; pick up and knit along right edge as for left side of scarf (approx 204 sts), PM, k33—approx 473 sts.

Rnd 1: (left edge) Sl 1 wyib, *p1, pfb; rep from * to next marker; (bottom edge) sl marker, sl 1 wyib, purl to next marker; (right edge) sl marker, sl 1 wyib, *p1, pfb; rep from * to next marker; (top edge) sl marker, sl 1 wyib, purl to end.

Rnd 2: *K1, yo, knit to next marker, yo, sl marker; rep from * 3 more times.

Rnd 3: *Sl 1 wyib, purl to next marker; rep from * 3 more times.

Rep Rnds 2 and 3 once more.

Next buttonhole rnd: K1, yo, knit to next marker, yo, sl marker, k1, yo, k2, [yo, k2tog, k4] 5 times, yo, k2tog, k1, yo, sl marker, *k1, yo, knit to next marker, yo; rep from * 2 more times.

Rep Rnd 2.

Rep Rnds 2 and 3 two more times.

Loosely BO all sts purlwise. Block to finished measurements. Weave in ends. Sew buttons opposite buttonholes.

Slip Stitch Chart

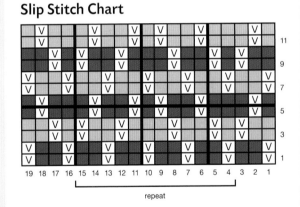

19 18 17 16 15 14 13 12 11 10 9 8 7 6 5 4 3 2 1

repeat

Stitch Key

☐ knit on RS, purl on WS

■ knit on RS, purl on WS

V sl 1 wyib

Note: Light gray indicates the first color, dark gray indicates the second color (colors vary depending on where you are in the pattern). Slipped stitches are shown in white to emphasize contrast between slipped stitches and knit or purled stitches in the same row.

Newkirk Intarsia Vest

DESIGNER: Carol J. Sulcoski   SKILL LEVEL: Intermediate

For a while I wanted to design a sweater that mixed a self-patterning yarn with a solid one. I decided to use the self-patterning yarn to create a decorative intarsia column, adding lots of color without having to buy multiple balls of yarn or weave in many ends. A rib pattern in the front builds in flexible fit for your curves. Although the model is wearing a small size for a cropped, close fit, opt for a larger size if you prefer more ease and a longer length.

INSTRUCTIONS

Front:

With larger needle and A, CO 41 (49, 57, 65, 73) sts, PM, CO 19 sts, PM, CO 41 (49, 57, 65, 73) sts—101 (117, 133, 149, 165) sts.

SET PAT AS FOLLOWS:

Row 1: K1, *k2, p2; rep from * to first marker, sl marker, k19, sl marker, **p2, k2; rep from ** to last st, k1.

Row 2: K1, *k4, p2, k2; rep from * to next marker, p19, **k2, p2, k4; rep from ** to last st, k1.

Row 3: Rep Row 1.

Row 4: K1, *p2, k6; rep from * to next marker, p19, **k6, p2; rep from ** to last st, k1.

Rows 5–8: Rep Rows 1–4.

FINISHED MEASUREMENTS

Chest: 32 (35, 39½, 44, 48½)"/81 (89, 100, 112, 123)cm (Ribbing pattern on front piece has a good deal of stretch giving flexibility in fit)

Length (total): 18 (19¼, 21, 22½, 14)"/46 (49, 53, 57, 61)cm

Length (from bottom edge to armhole): 10½ (11¾, 13, 14¼, 15½)"/27 (30, 33, 36, 39)cm

---

MATERIALS AND TOOLS

Regia Extra Twist Merino (75% superwash wool, 25% polyamide; 1.75oz/50g = 230yd/209m): (A), 3 (3, 4, 4, 5) skeins, color brown #9360—approx 850yd/914m of solid-colored fingering weight yarn (1)

Noro Taiyo Sock (50% cotton, 17% wool, 17% nylon, 16% silk; 3.5oz/100g = 462yd/422m): (B), 1 skein, color #6—approx 100yd/90m of self-patterning fingering weight yarn (1)

Knitting needles: 3.25mm (size 3 U.S.) needles or size to obtain gauge

2.75mm (size 2 U.S.) 16" circular needle or one size smaller than above

Stitch markers (optional)

Tapestry needle

GAUGE

28 sts/36 rows = 4"/10cm in St st. Note: Gauge is measured in St st because the stretch of ribbing makes it difficult to measure accurately.

Always take time to check your gauge.

JOIN B AS FOLLOWS:

Row 9: K1, *k2, p2; rep from * to first marker, with B, k19, join second ball of A and work **p2, k2; rep from ** to last st, k1.

Row 10: K1, *k4, p2, k2; rep from * to next marker, with B, p19, with other ball of A, **k2, p2, k4; rep from ** to last st, k1.

Row 11: Rep Row 9.

Row 12: K1, *p2, k6; rep from * to next marker, with B, p19, with A, **k6, p2; rep from ** to last st, k1.

Rep Rows 9–12 until front measures 10½ (11¾, 13, 14¼, 15½)"/27 (30, 33, 36, 39)cm from beg or desired length to armhole, ending with a WS row.

Note: Keep pattern correct at all times as you work decreases and bind off sts for armholes and neckline.

DECREASE FOR ARMHOLES:

Keeping pattern correct, BO 6 (6, 7, 7, 8) sts at the beg of next 2 rows; then BO 2 sts at the beg of the next 4 (4, 6, 8, 8) rows, then dec 1 st at each end of the next 3 RS rows-- 75 (91, 101, 113, 127) sts.

Now begin working neckline:

Next row (WS): Keeping pattern correct, work over first 28 (36, 41, 47, 54) sts for right shoulder, BO center 19 sts, work to end for left shoulder—28 (36, 41, 47, 54) sts for each shoulder.

Working on left shoulder sts only, dec 1 st at armhole edge on next 2 (4, 5, 5, 7) RS rows, and AT THE SAME TIME, BO 0 (0, 2, 2, 3) sts at neck edge every other row 0 (0, 3, 4, 6) times, then dec 1 st at neck edge every row a total of 11 (17, 14, 15, 9) times—15 (15, 16, 19, 20) sts rem.

Cont without further dec, if necessary, until armhole measures 7½ (7½, 8, 8¼, 8½)"/19 (19, 20, 21, 22)cm. BO all sts.

Rejoin yarn and work right shoulder to match, reversing all shaping.

BACK:

With larger needle and A, CO 114 (122, 138, 154, 170) sts.

Row 1 (RS): K1, *k2, p2; rep from * to last st, k1.

Row 2: K1, *k2, p2, k4; rep from * to last st, k1.

Row 3: Rep Row 1.

Row 4: K1, *k6, p2; rep from* to last st, k1.

Rows 5–8: Rep Rows 1–4.

Change to St st, inc 0 (6, 4, 6, 4) sts evenly across first row—114 (128, 142, 160, 174) sts.

Cont in St st until back measures 10½ (11¾, 13, 14¼, 15½)"/27 (30, 33, 36, 39)cm or same as front to armholes.

DECREASE FOR ARMHOLES:

Keeping pattern correct, BO 6 (6, 7, 7, 8) sts at the beg of the next 2 rows; then BO 2 sts at the beg of the next 4 (4, 6, 8, 8) rows, then dec 1 st at each end of the next 5 (7, 8, 8, 10) RS rows—84 (94, 100, 114, 122) sts.

Cont working without further dec until back measures 5½ (5½, 6, 6¼, 6½)"/14 (14, 15, 16, 17)cm from beg of armhole shaping, end with a WS row.

SHAPE NECK:

Next row (RS): K33 (36, 40, 45, 47) for right shoulder, BO center 18 (22, 20, 24, 28) sts, knit to end for left shoulder.

Working on left shoulder sts only:

Next row: Purl.

Next row: BO 2 (3, 3, 3, 3) sts, knit to end—31 (33, 37, 42, 44) sts.

Next row: Purl.

Rep these 2 rows 8 (6, 7, 8, 8) times—15 (15, 16, 18, 20) sts.

Cont without dec, if necessary, until armhole measures 7½ (7½, 8, 8¼, 8½)"/ 19 (19, 20, 21, 22)cm, or until shoulder strap is even with corresponding front shoulder strap.

BO all sts.

Rejoin yarn on other side and work right shoulder to match, reversing all shaping.

FINISHING

Weave in ends and block as desired.

Sew side seams and shoulder straps together.

Neckband:

With smaller circular needle and A, and beg at left shoulder seam, pick up and knit approx 46 (50, 54, 58, 62) sts down left neck, 19 sts across center front neck, 46 (50, 54, 58, 62) sts up right neck, and 73 (77, 85, 93, 101) sts across back neck—184 (196, 212, 228, 244) sts. PM and join for working in the rnd.

Work 8 rnds in 2x2 Rib.

BO all sts in rib.

Armholes (both the same):

With smaller circular needle and A, and beg at underarm, pick up and knit approx 108 (112, 116, 120, 128) sts around armhole. PM and join for working in the rnd. Work 8 rnds in 2x2 Rib.

BO all sts in rib. Weave in ends.

Schematic

2 (2, 2¼, 2¾, 3)" / 5 (5, 6, 7, 7) cm

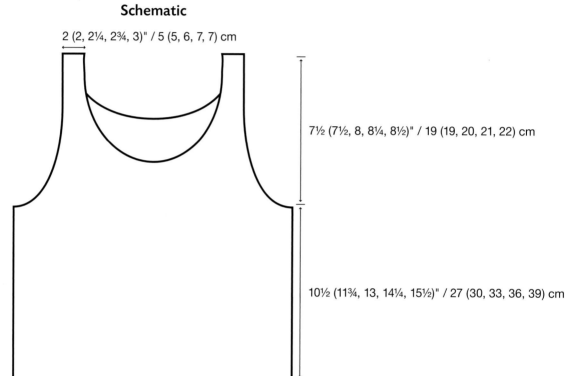

7½ (7½, 8, 8¼, 8½)" / 19 (19, 20, 21, 22) cm

10½ (11¾, 13, 14¼, 15½)" / 27 (30, 33, 36, 39) cm

16 (17½, 19¾, 22, 24¼)" / 41 (45, 50, 56, 62) cm

about the author

CAROL J. SULCOSKI is a former attorney turned knitting designer and hand-dyer. She is author of *Knitting Socks With Handpainted Yarns* (Interweave Press, 2009) and co-author of *Knit So Fine: Knitting with Skinny Yarns* (Interweave Press, 2008). Her designs have been published in *Vogue Knitting, Knit Simple, St-Denis Magazine, KnitScene,* and various other books and magazines. Her technical articles frequently appear in *Vogue Knitting.* She also founded Black Bunny Fibers (www.blackbunnyfibers.com), an independent dyeing business creating unique handpainted yarns and fibers, and her patterns can be found on Ravelry and Patternfish. She lives outside Philadelphia with her family.

about the contributors

VÉRONIK AVERY

Véronik Avery is the owner of St-Denis Yarns and the author of *Knitting 24/7* (Stewart, Tabori & Chang, 2010) and *Knitting Classic Style* (STC, 2007). Her work has appeared in over 30 books and publications such as *Weekend Knitting* (STC, 2009), *Handknit Holidays* (STC, 2005), *Reversible Knitting* (STC, 2009), *Vogue Knitting, Interweave Knits* and others. She lives outside Montreal with her family, where she edits and publishes the bi-annual *St-Denis Magazine.* For more information, visit www.stdenisyarns.com.

BARBARA J. BROWN

Barb Brown is a designer and lifelong knitter, living in Alberta, Canada. Her book, *Knitting Knee-Highs: Sock Styles from Classic to Contemporary* (Krause), was released in February 2011. Her designs have appeared in *Vogue Knitting, Yarn Forward, The Knitter* and other publications. Barb also teaches at various community colleges, fiber events, retreats and yarn shops.

ANMIRYAM BUDNER

Anmiryam began knitting in her 30s and hasn't looked back. Simple or complicated, it all appeals and the hardest part is making a decision about what to knit next and what yarns need to live in her stash.

ERIKA FLORY

Erika Flory has been designing knitwear for babies and toddlers for over 20 years, and offers patterns and kits on her website, www.kidknits.biz. Her designs have appeared in the knitting webzines *KnitNet, For the Love of Yarn, Knotions, The Daily Knitter* and *Petite Purls,* as well as in the WEBS online and print catalogs for Valley Yarns, and for Pisgah Yarn & Dyeing. Her book of patterns, *Head to Toe Knits: 23 Designs to Knit for Baby* (2008), is available through lulu.com. Not a day goes by that she doesn't touch yarn.

RUTH GARCIA-ALCANTUD

Ruth pairs up classic elegant details with bright colors to cheer up any rainy day. She designs and teaches from her studio in the south of England, where she moved from her native country of Spain. You can visit her at www.rockandpurl.com/blog for details about her designs and workshops.

TANIS GRAY

Tanis Gray lives on Capitol Hill in Washington, DC with her mechanical engineer husband, infant son, and lazy pug. Tanis is the author of *Knit Local* (Sixth & Spring, 2011) and *Capitol Knits* (Create Space, 2012). She has over 250 published designs. Find out more at www.tanisknits.com.

LAURA GRUTZECK

Laura Grutzeck is a knitwear designer and librarian who lives in Philadelphia with her husband and a pack of wild dogs. Her work has appeared in such publications as *Interweave Knits*, *Vogue Knitting*, and *St-Denis Magazine*, and she is one of the co-authors of *Knit So Fine: Knitting with Skinny Yarns* (Interweave Press, 2008).

FRANKLIN HABIT

Franklin Habit is a Chicago-based designer of handknits and the author of *It Itches: A Stash of Knitting Cartoons* (Interweave Press, 2008). He contributes regularly to major fiber arts publications and is the proprietor of the popular knitting blog *The Panopticon* (www.the-panopticon.blogspot.com).

HUNTER HAMMERSEN

Scandalous though it is to admit, Hunter Hammersen didn't really like knitting the first time she tried it. She wasn't too keen on it the second time around either. It wasn't until the third time (and the discovery of knitted socks) that she was properly smitten. A year later she realized she could make up her own patterns and her fate was sealed. Her work has been featured in *Knitty* and *Knitcircus*. Her first book, *Silk Road Socks* (Cooperative Press), was published in 2011 and her second, *The Knitter's Curiosity Cabinet*, in 2012. You can find her at www.violentlydomestic.com, where she continues to revel in the glory of really comfy socks.

WENDY D. JOHNSON

Wendy D. Johnson is a lifelong knitter who has maintained the popular knitting blog www.wendyknits.net since April 2002. She is the author of *Wendy Knits: My Never-Ending Adventures in Yarn* (Plume, 2006), *Socks From the Toe Up* (Potter Craft, 2009), *Toe-Up Socks for Every Body* (Potter Craft, 2010), and *Wendy Knits Lace* (Potter Craft, 2011).

MELISSA MORGAN-OAKES

Melissa Morgan-Oakes was taught to crochet, tat, and sew at an early age by women who encouraged her to work without commercial patterns. Looking for new challenges, she taught herself to spin and knit, designing patterns for her handspun yarns as she went. She lives on a small chicken farm in Western Massachusetts with her husband, a very large dog, and a very small dog. Melissa is the author of *2-at-a-Time Socks* (Storey, 2007), *Toe-Up 2-at-a-Time Socks* (Storey, 2010), and *Teach Yourself Visually Circular Knitting* (Wiley, 2011).

ELIZABETH MORRISON

Elizabeth Morrison lives with her husband and two sons in Madison, Wisconsin. She learned to knit as a child, but it didn't really take until the late 1980s. See more of her work at www.sweaterstudio.com or find her on Ravelry as ElizabethSABLE.

BROOKE NICO

Brooke began her designing activities by sewing her own wardrobe, inspired by drape and color. She brought her talents to knitting almost 10 years ago, first exploring modular construction, then lace. In 2006, Brooke opened Kirkwood Knittery, a local yarn shop located in St. Louis, MO. As a dedicated teacher, Brooke guides knitters through the intricacies of techniques to make their projects as polished as possible.

knitting abbreviations

ABBR.	DESCRIPTION	ABBR.	DESCRIPTION	ABBR.	DESCRIPTION	ABBR.	DESCRIPTION
[]	work instructions within brackets as many times as directed	dpn	double pointed needle(s)	p or P	purl	sl st	slip stitch(es)
()	work instructions within parentheses as many times as directed	foll	follow/follows/following	pfb	purl through front & back loops of stitch; 1 st increased	sl1k	slip 1 knitwise
**	repeat instructions following the asterisks as directed	g	gram	pat(s) or patt	patterns	sl1p	slip 1 purlwise
*	repeat instructions following the single asterisk as directed	inc	increase/increases/increasing	PM	place marker	ssk	slip, slip, knit these 2 stitches together—a decrease
"	inches	k or K	knit	prev	previous	sssk	slip, slip, slip, knit 3 stitches together
alt	alternate	kfb	knit through front & back loops of stitch; 1 st increased	psso	pass slipped stitch over	st(s)	stitch(es)
ap-prox	approximately	k2tog	knit 2 stitches together	p2tog	purl 2 stitches together	St st	stockinette stitch/stocking stitch
beg	begin/beginning	K3tog	knit 3 stitches together	rem	remain/remaining	tbl	through back loop
bet	between	LH	left hand	rep	repeat(s)	tog	together
BO	bind off	m	meter(s)	rev St st	reverse stockinette stitch	WS	wrong side
CC	contrasting color	MC	main color	RH	right hand	wyib	with yarn in back
cm	centimeter(s)	mm	millimeter(s)	rnd(s)	round(s)	wyif	with yarn in front
cn	cable needle	M1	make 1 stitch	RS	right side	yd(s)	yard(s)
CO	cast on	M1R	make 1 st slanting to right; 1 st increased	skp	slip, knit, pass stitch over—one stitch decreased	yo	yarn over
cont	continue	M1L	make 1 st slanting to left; 1 st increased	sk2p	slip 1, knit 2 together, pass slip stitch over the knit 2 together; 2 stiches have been decreased		
dec	decrease/decreases/decreasing	oz	ounce(s)	sl	slip		

yarn sources

ArtYarns (Cashmere Sock,
Silk Lace)
39 Westmoreland Ave.
White Plains, NY 10606
(914) 428-0333
www.artyarns.com

Black Bunny Fibers (Bamberino
Sock, Cashmerino Sock, Falkland
Softsilk Sock, Plump, Softsilk
Sock)
www.blackbunnyfibers.com

Classic Elite Yarns (Alpaca Sox)
16 Esquire Rd.
Unit 2
North Billerica, MA
1-800-343-0308
www.classiceliteyarns.com

Crystal Palace Yarns (Sausalito &
Mini Solid)
Straw Into Gold, Inc.
160 23rd St.
Richmond, CA 94804
www.straw.com

Garnstudio (Drops Delight)
DROPS DESIGN A/S
Jerikoveien 10 A
NO-1067 Oslo, Norway
47 23 30 32 20
www.garnstudio.com

Koigu Wool Co. (KPM, KPPM)
Box 158
Chatsworth , Ontario
N0H 1G0 Canada
1-888-765-WOOL
www.koigu.com

Lion Brand (Sock-Ease)
135 Kero Rd.
Carlstadt, NJ 07072
800-661-7551
www.lionbrand.com

The Loopy Ewe (Solid Series)
2720 Council Tree Ave.
Suite 255
Fort Collins, CO 80525
www.theloopyewe.com

Lorna's Laces (Shepherd Sock)
4229 N. Honore St.
Chicago,IL 60613
773-935-3803
www.lornaslaces.net

Louet North America
(GEMS Fingering)
3425 Hands Rd.
Prescott, Ontario
K0E 1T0 Canada
613-925-4502
www.louet.com

MadelineTosh Yarns
(Tosh Sock)
7515 Benbrook Pkwy
Benbrook, TX 76126
817-249-3066
www.madelinetosh.com

Malabrigo (Sock)
786-866-6187
www.malabrigoyarn.com

Noro (Taiyo Sock)
Knitting Fever, Inc.
PO Box 336
315 Bayview Ave.
Amityville, NY 11701
516-546-3600
www.knittingfever.com

Opal (Huntdertwasser 2)
Tutto-Opal-Isager
10 Domingo Rd.
Santa Fe, NM 87508
877-603-OPAL (6725)
www.opalsockyarn.com

Quince and Co. (Tern)
85 York St.
Portland, ME 04101
www.quinceandco.com

The Sanguine Gryphon
(Bugga Sock)
*Note: The Sanguine Gryphon
has closed and been
re-organized into:*
www.cephalopodyarns.com
www.verdantgryphon.com

Shibui (Staccato Sock)
Shibui Knits, LLC.
1500 NW 18th St., Suite 110
Portland, OR 97209
503-595-5898
www.shibuiknits.com

Skacel (Zauberball,
Step Classic)
Skacel Collection, Inc.
800-255-1278
www.skacelknitting.com

Socks That Rock
Blue Moon Fiber Arts, Inc.
56587 Mollenhour Rd.
Scappoose, OR 97056
866-802-9687
www.bluemoonfiberarts.com

Spud & Chloe (Fine)
Blue Sky Alpacas
Attn: Spud & Chloë
P.O. Box 88
Cedar, MN 55011
www.spudandchloe.com

St-Denis Yarns (Boréale)
www.stdenisyarns.com
info@stdenisyarns.com

Swan's Island (Fingering Wt.)
231 Atlantic Highway (Route 1)
Northport, ME 04849
888-526-9526
www.swansislandblankets.com

Universal Yarns (Poems Sock,
Marathon Socks)
284 Ann St.
Concord, NC 28025
877- 864-9276
www.universalyarns.com

Valley Yarns (Charlemont)
WEBS: America's Yarn Store
75 Service Center Rd.
Northampton, MA 01060
800-FOR-WEBS
www.yarn.com

Westminster Fibers (Regia sock
yarns, including Regia 4-ply
 Regia Merino Extra Twist)
8 Shelter Dr.
Greer, SC 29650
us.knitsmc.com/regia

Wollemeise (100% Merino
Superwash)
Rohrspatz & Wollmeise
Birkengrund 29
85276 Pfaffenhofen
Germany
49-0-8441-78-93-80
www.wollmeise-yarnshop.de

dedication

For Shirley, the best. mother. ever.
And in memory of my dad, who was the first author in the family.

acknowledgments

First, great thanks to my agent Linda Roghaar; she told me she'd find a home for this book, and darn, if she wasn't right. Likewise, thanks to Thom O'Hearn at Lark for recognizing the potential in my proposal. I was fortunate enough to have two outstanding Lark editors work on this book: Valerie Shrader got me off to a rock-solid start, then handed me off to Thom, who helped make the book the best it could be with his thoughtful, teal-colored edits.

This book gave me the chance to work with some of my favorite people in the knitting industry: the designers who contributed projects to this book. Many of them are dear friends and all were a joy to work with. With so many talented people in the industry, I could have filled many more books with interesting, beautiful projects—and hope to in the future—but this particular group knocked me out with their professionalism, enthusiasm, and skill.

Likewise, I cannot say enough good things about ace photographer and stylist Carrie Bostick Hoge. Her photographs reveal the beauty of each project with elegance and style, and her charming personality made the process fun. Thanks, too, to the absolutely gorgeous models: Kim, Lida, Marena, Evan, Nyanen, Imogen and Dennis, and of course my own little miss, Grace.

Thanks to my technical editor, K.J. Hay, for her terrific technical editing, and to Kara Plikaitis for creating the book's lovely design.

Knitting many projects on a short deadline often requires the use of test knitters; much thanks to Sally Watson Cushmore, Elizabeth Durand, Mindy Hook and Heather Vance. Thanks to Craig Rosenfeld & the staff of Loop for their enthusiasm and support—particularly with last-minute yarn needs.

A shout-out to Jen Neuhoff of Northfound, for technical and graphics help above and beyond the call of duty. An amazing graphics designer who is also a knitter is rare and helpful indeed.

Thank you to Nanette and Craig for allowing us to take photographs in their beautiful home; to Bliss and Black Parrot Boutiques, in Portland, ME, for generously lending items for our models to wear during the photo shoots; and to Spool Sewing, Philadelphia, for the loan of several gorgeous quilts.

A special thank-you to my dear knitting & fb friends. I am fortunate to have been befriended by an amazing group of talented, warm-hearted, funny people—you know who you are and I couldn't bear to be without you.

And of course I saved the best for last: my beloved family. My children James, Nick, and Grace were always encouraging and their pride in my work makes my heart burst. I'm sorry for all those times I had to say, "later," because I was working. To Charcoal, for being the best, most snuggly bunny ever. To my husband, Tom, whose love and support means more than I can say.

recommended reading

If you'd like to learn more about sock knitting, the following books will get you started:

Brown, Barbara. *Knitting Knee-Highs: Sock Styles from Classic to Contemporary*. Cincinnati, OH: Krause, 2011.

Bush, Nancy. *Folk Socks*. Loveland, CO: Interweave Press, 1994 and revised edition 2011.

Cookie A. *Knit Sock Love*. CA: One Leg Press, 2010.

Johnson, Wendy. *Socks From the Toe Up*. New York: Potter Craft, 2009.

--------.*Toe-Up Socks for Every Body*. New York: Potter Craft, 2010.

Kopp, Linda. *The Joy of Socks*. New York: Lark Books, 2009.

Morgan-Oakes, Melissa. *2-at-a-Time Socks*. North Adams, MA: Storey, 2007.

--------.*Toe-Up 2-at-a-Time Socks*. North Adams, MA: Storey, 2010.

Vogue Knitting: The Ultimate Sock Book. New York: Sixth & Spring, 2007.

If you'd like to learn more about the issue of pooling, particularly as it relates to sock knitting, you'll want to read my earlier book, *Knitting Socks With Handpainted Yarns* (Interweave Press, 2009).

For more about sock yarn, and yarn in general, Clara Parkes' trifecta—*The Knitter's Book of Yarn* (2007), *The Knitter's Book of Wool* (2009), and *The Knitter's Book of Socks* (2011), all from Potter Craft—are unmatched for their thoroughness and readability.

index

It's all on **www.larkcrafts.com**

Daily blog posts featuring needlearts, jewelry and beading, and all things crafty

Free, downloadable **projects** and **how-to videos**

Calls for artists and **book submissions**

A free **e-newsletter** announcing new and exciting books

...and a place to celebrate the **creative spirit**